# French Country Crafts

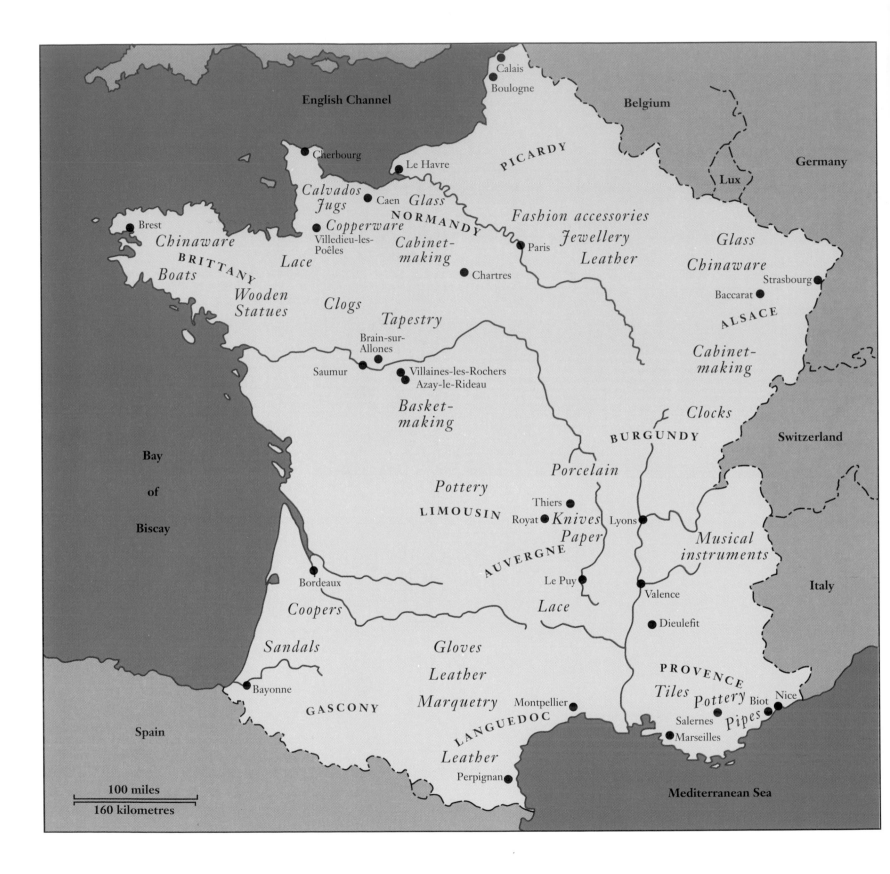

English Channel

Calais
Boulogne

Belgium

PICARDY

Germany

Lux

Cherbourg

Le Havre

*Calvados Jugs*

Caen *Glass*

NORMANDY

*Fashion accessories*
*Jewellery*
*Leather*

*Glass*
*Chinaware*

Strasbourg

Brest

*Chinaware*

BRITTANY

*Lace*

*Copperware*

Villedieu-les-Poêles

*Cabinet-making*

Paris

Baccarat

ALSACE

*Boats*

*Wooden Statues*

*Clogs*

*Tapestry*

Chartres

*Cabinet-making*

Brain-sur-Allones

Saumur

Villaines-les-Rochers
Azay-le-Rideau

*Clocks*

Bay

of

Biscay

*Basket-making*

BURGUNDY

*Porcelain*

Switzerland

*Pottery*

LIMOUSIN

Thiers

Royat *Knives*

Lyons

*Paper*

*Musical instruments*

Italy

Bordeaux

*Coopers*

AUVERGNE

Le Puy

Valence

*Sandals*

*Gloves*

*Lace*

Dieulefit

Bayonne

GASCONY

*Leather*

*Marquetry*

Montpellier

LANGUEDOC

PROVENCE

*Tiles* *Pottery* Biot Nice

Salernes

*Pipes*

Spain

Marseilles

*Leather*

Perpignan

Mediterranean Sea

100 miles

160 kilometres

# MARIE-PIERRE MOINE

# French Country Crafts

## PHOTOGRAPHS
## HUGH PALMER

CASSELL

A CASSELL BOOK

First published 1993
by Cassell
Villiers House, 41/47 Strand
London WC2N 5 JE

Distributed in Australia by
Capricorn Link (Australia) Pty Ltd
PO Box 665, Lane Cove, NSW 2066

**British Library Cataloguing-in-Publication Data**
A catalogue record for this book is available from the British Library

ISBN 0-304-34120-7

Typeset in Monotype Janson by
MS Filmsetting Limited, Frome, Somerset

Printed and bound in Great Britain
by Bath Colour Books

*Photo credits* Baccarat 106–7, 109, 110–11, 112; Réunion des Musées Nationaux,
France 8, 10, 11, 12, 13, 15

This book is dedicated to the memory of
my grand-father, Alfred Richet
(1893–1992).

# Acknowledgments

First of all, my thanks go to Hugh Palmer whose photographs convey so much about the artisans we visited. I am also grateful to Hugh for being such fun to travel and work with – and for patiently putting up with any navigational shortcomings.

I was received kindly and helpfully by all the people I interviewed in the course of writing this book: R. Augé-Laribé; M. Beillonet and Mme Liebens; Mme Bergamo; Chantal Burns and Alexandre Chodzko; Michèle Cosnier; Charles Courrieu; Etienne Dullin; Charles Fresneau; Marcel Harlais; Roger Hérisset; Gilbert Hervieux and Olivier Glet; Mireille Juteau; Alain Kirch; Danièle and Jean Lechaczynski; Claude Le Corre; Yves Le Goupil; Frédérique Leperré; Bernard Lissague; Claude Metezeau; Claude, Nicolas and Frédéric Morin; Mmes Noir and Harvois; Marie-Catherine Nobécourt; Bruno Pottier; Bernard Salvador, Mylène Salvador and Fabienne Ros; Mme Sismondini; Nicolas and Olivier Sourdive; Alain Vagh; Mireille Verdenet.

I should also like to acknowledge with thanks the generous assistance of Brigitte Lozza and her colleagues at the Musée des Arts et Traditions Populaires, of the SEMA, Meilleurs Ouvriers de France and Association Ouvrière des Compagnons du Devoir, and in London of Françoise Peretti of Peretti Communications.

A very special thanks goes to Michèle Richet who tirelessly sent me relevant information and was always willing to answer questions.

Thanks go to Wolf and Shirley Rilla for their welcome and hospitality at Le Moulin de la Camandoule when Hugh and I stayed there in loco Colin, to Pierre Moine who let us treat Le Boisseau like a hotel while we were working in the region and to Françoise Moine for her support. Finally my gratitude goes to my friend and editorial accomplice, Lewis Esson, and to Colin MacIvor who always finds *le mot juste* (or the right joke) when my spirits flag.

# Contents

# Introduction
## The ancient crafts of France

In spite of all the pressures of the modern world, the cult of craftsmanship remains intensely alive in France today. Perhaps this tells us something of the innate passion for individuality and private workmanship that must be at the very heart of being French. A number of factors have helped the artisan tradition endure to this day. One is the sheer size of the country, stretching as it does from the cool dairy land of northern Europe to the warm olive oil shores of the Mediterranean. Different climates meant different ways of life and therefore a wealth of different local crafts and customs. Having proudly nurtured its own unique character and traditions, each region of France is still convinced of its secret superiority. It is no wonder that what the English call parochialism and the French *esprit de clocher* is frankly derogatory in English, while in French it is said with a tolerant smile. In the last decade of the twentieth century regionality thrives in the country as a whole. It never was seriously endangered by France's industrial revolution, which took place significantly later than England's in the nineteenth century and was far less drastic in its consequences. It happened gradually, in a piecemeal fashion, in some parts of the country only with the utmost reluctance.

Perhaps the main reason behind the, by and large healthy, survival of its artisan crafts has been France's long history of commercial protectionism. From early medieval times, powerful occupational associations were set up to defend the interests of craftsmen.

These authentic photographs of late nineteenth-century France recall a world in which hand crafts rather than machine production were the norm. In France industrialization developed more patchily than elsewhere, and regional crafts skills survived vigorously. *From top left* bundling split and trimmed laths in the Forest of Montmorency, north of Paris; slate dressers in the Tarn, southern France; polishing knives in Thiers, Auvergne; hammering out a cauldron, Tarn; clog-sellers in Concarneau, Brittany.

### From early guilds to the end of the corporations

From the ninth century onwards, artisans started to come together in *guildes* and *confréries* (guilds and brotherhoods). In the early days these were charitable associations with strong religious overtones set up to protect the common interests of their members. Each had a patron saint who was duly honoured at regular festivals, notably Saint Joseph, the universal patron of carpenters and wood-workers. Some of the traditional rituals of the *confréries* are still part of French folklore.

From the twelfth century, with the development of towns and an increasing demand for skilled work, artisans became more specialized – masons, carpenters, cabinet-makers, potters, tanners, blacksmiths, cobblers... The

A potter at work in the Drôme, southeastern France.

rules and regulations governing the various crafts multiplied. On the one hand customers had to be satisfied that what they were ordering was of a certain standard and on the other the profession itself, *le métier*, had to be properly organized – and defended against potential competition by outsiders. Protectionism was born.

The minimum duration and the conditions of apprenticeship were laid out. Only *maîtres*, master-craftsmen, were allowed to practise and employ apprentices and workers. In order to qualify for a *maîtrise* an artisan had to fashion a *chef d'oeuvre*, a masterpiece (both the French *chef d'oeuvre* and the German *Meisterstück* seem to have kept a slightly stronger, more emphatic meaning than the somewhat devalued masterpiece, but one should not rush to conclusions…).

In any town or city, candidates for the *maîtrise* had to satisfy a jury of their peers and fellow craftsmen. The new *maître* had to pay a hefty admission fee (and eventually also a levy to the chronically improverished Crown) which proved prohibitive for many and sometimes resulted in creating a virtual monopoly. Only the sons of wealthy enough *maîtres* could afford access and thousands of dissatisfied qualified workers wandered off to seek their fortunes elsewhere. Many joined a *société compagnonnique*, a group of like-minded independent artisans. These 'alternative' craft movements were never as influential as the established guilds, *maîtrises* and corporations during the *Ancien Régime*. Yet, unlike them, they have survived to this day (see below) after a difficult, occasionally quasi-clandestine, period in the nineteenth century.

From product specification and prescribed holidays to the rights of a deceased *maître*'s widow and children, increasingly complex statutes gradually began to regulate every aspect of working conditions. At the same time crafts and trades were classified into a multitude of different *métiers* (some practically indistinguishable) which were grouped into seemingly arbitrary classes. Each class had a different tax scale. For instance in Dijon towards the end of the reign of Louis XIV, with the exception of tanners and bookbinders, the first class included no artisans – only merchants. Tapestry-workers, saddlers, shoemakers and pewter-smiths featured amongst the second hand. One class down the ladder were glaziers, coopers, cabinet-makers, painters and sculptors. Bottom came basket-makers, carpenters, weavers, and stonemasons, to list but a few.

The complicated system of craft associations (the word *corporation* only began to be widely used in the eighteenth century) was naturally open to excesses and corruption. Time and time again over the centuries there were calls for its abolition. Freedom of work was one of the fundamental tenets of the French Revolution, and craft associations with all their regulations and classifications were finally abolished in 1791 along with the rest of the institutions of the *Ancien Régime*.

## Colbert and commercial protectionism

The constant efforts of generations of French kings to control their land was both a curse and a boon for the country's *artisanat*. The Crown's power to ban craft and trade associations when it felt serious trouble was brewing was one such mixed blessing. Completely on the negative side was its enduring habit of levying emergency taxes whenever the royal coffers were depleted. The taxes were crippling, usually unfairly aimed and always bitterly resented.

Much more positive for the development of French crafts was the doctine of commercial protectionism actively pursued in the seventeenth and eighteenth centuries. The best exponent of the principle at a crucial period in French history was Colbert during the twenty-two years of his ministry (1661–1683).

The ground had been prepared for him by a general awakening of interest in economics and by the efforts of his great ministerial predecessors. Sully, Richelieu and Mazarin. Montchrestien's *Traité de l'Oeconomie Politique* (1615) wanted 'the country to supply the country'. There was a belief that, since France was a country rich in natural resourcces and nearly self-sufficient, it should manufacture all its everyday and luxury goods at home – thus employing its workless poor and keeping its gold and silver within the kingdom.

Sharpening knives in a Paris street, *c* 1900.

On the home front, this was very good news for *artisanat*. It meant that the development of crafts and luxury goods was actively encouraged. Colbert took every opportunity to promote home and local manufacturing. He made new machinery such as looms more widely available, tried to reduce the workers' direct tax burden, set up strict quality regulations, levied extra duties on imports and attempted to standardize weights and measures.

More creatively still, where native expertise and craftsmanship were lacking, he did not hesitate in hiring in artisans from abroad. An interesting example of his shrewd approach is the lace workshop Colbert created in Alençon in 1665 (see page 117). With an acute sense for the 'unique selling proposition' he brought in Venetian lace-makers to help create a particularly fine needle lace that was to be unique to Alençon and good enough to rival pieces produced in Flanders or England. The French *produit de luxe* was born. Not all of Colbert's measures were successful but his influence has been long-lasting and significant. Very appropriately, the leaders of France's contemporary luxury goods industry have named an award of excellence after him, *le Prix Colbert*.

## *Compagnonnage*, technical traditions and the spirit of independent craftsmanship

Even though the last of the medieval guilds and corporations were finally abolished during the Revolution in 1791, the old alternative system of *Compagnonnage* still has an important role to play in the *artisanat* of today's France. *Sociétés de Compagnonnage* began as associations of dedicated wandering craftsmen. Legend has it that the origins of the movement go back to the building of King Solomon's temple … Less picturesquely far-fetched is the widely held view that *Compagnonnage* started on the construction sites of the great European cathedrals and monasteries. Craftsmen flocked to the cities where the new churches were being built. There they were likely to be hired by rich prelates and powerful lords intent on demonstrating their own proud independence. And it was also there that they were best able to master their skills: from geometry to medicine, the sum of knowledge of the civilized world, the treatises of the Ancients were kept by monks in abbeys and monasteries.

The early *compagnons* were primarily carpenters and stonemasons involved in the quest for the perfect Line, *l'Art du Trait*. To this day the building trades play a very important part in the movement and mastering the art of the line has remained a dominant preoccupation. The word *trait* still sometimes features in the working pseudonym a *compagnon* ritually adopts when he is received into the fellowship and introduced to the trade secrets: *Nantais-l'Ami-du-Trait* (the man from Nantes who loves the Line). Names often refer to the birthplace of the *compagnon* or to a virtue which he admires – *Agennais-la-Clef des Coeurs* (he from Agen key to all hearts), *Breton-le-Courageux* (Breton the Brave), *Avignonnais la Vertu* (the chosen name of Agricol Perdiguier, a leading figure of the movement in the nineteenth century whose tomb in the Père Lachaise cemetery in Paris is still honoured every year on 1st November).

Not surprisingly the Establishment of the thirteenth and fourteenth centuries became a little uneasy at the willingness of artisans to wander off – mobility being a means of becoming better informed, freer and potentially more troublesome. Soon statutes expressly forbade workers to leave their employer without prior agreement. But, by 1420, *Compagnonnage* had become a fact of life – tolerated rather than officially recognized. The work of cobblers was defined in an ordnance by Charles VI. It describes *compagnons* and journeymen 'from different countries and speaking different languages going about their business' in Troyes 'working and learning from each other' – an idyllic vision of Europe still, in our post-Maastricht era.

In order to be received into a society and to become a *compagnon*, a journeyman of old had to accomplish a masterpiece while travelling around the length and breadth of France. This demonstrated his technical expertise

An embroiderer works by a window in the Vosges, eastern France.

Lace-makers in the Livradois, Auvergne, central France.

A traditional spinning wheel, late nineteenth century.

and also his fortitude. The quasi-spiritual dimension is an important one. The novelist George Sand referred to the *Compagnonnage* as '*cette chevalerie ouvrière*', this caste of knightly hand-workers. A favourite story amongst *compagnons* tells of three men all engaged in the same work on a cathedral building site. A passer-by asks them each the same question: 'What are you doing?' 'I am cutting a stone,' says the first man. 'I am earning a living,' replies the second. The third man answers, 'I am building a cathedral.' He of course is a *compagnon*... Masterpieces have included the wrought-iron gates of the Place Stanislas in Nancy and, more recently, in 1986, the renovation work on the Statue of Liberty. This involved a team of 10 iron-smiths and metal-workers who spent the best part of a year faithfully restoring Bartholdi's original work.

Gone are the days when the journeyman did his *Tour de France* on foot with a knapsack and a walking stick, always travelling with the sun, but training, *la formation*, is still based on the traditional principle of journeying from place to place. There are now three main *Compagnonnage* associations, *Association Ouvrière des Compagnons du Devoir*, *Fédération compagnonnique des Métiers du Bâtiment* and *Union compagnonnique des Devoirs*, each with a different political shade and slightly different objectives. All put a strong emphasis on training. For example, future *compagnons du Devoir* stay in one of a network of 100 or so houses – *maisons*. There are no women companions, but a house-mother, *une mère*, is in charge of the material running of each house and of the well-being of its inmates. Apprentices and aspiring companions live, study and practise their skills in a given house for 6 months to a year before moving onto another *maison*. Paid work placements are arranged for apprentices and they are encouraged to study for state exams. Throughout their training, they are helped and supervised by older *compagnons*.

At the end of the day, a new *compagnon* still has to produce a *chef d'oeuvre* – also called *travail de réception*, a prestigious admission work. He is then admitted to the fellowship in a ritual ceremony. Like his predecessors, he is expected to be a truly qualified professional craftsman, to keep alive the movement's traditions and to pass on the benefits of his experience to the next generation of *compagnons*.

Probably the most enjoyable overall introduction to the spirit of French craftsmanship is to be found in Tours. There in the heart of the old city close to the Loire is the *Musée du Compagnonnage*. Worth a detour according to Michelin, it is housed in and around the old dormitory of the monks of the Abbaye Saint-Julien. A delightful sign tells you that you have come to the right place. Within the wrought-iron outline of France as a frame, it shows two men toasting each other. They are standing with their drinking arms interlinked in the traditional stance of blood brothers.

In addition to historical artefacts, many of them gems of folk art, illustrating the legends and the *petite et grande histoire* of the *Compagnonnage* movement, the museum is home to a magnificent collection of masterpieces.

Sign of the Musée du Compagnonnage, Tours.

The various crafts are all represented: weavers and basket-makers, with a stunning osier horse and an impressive bust of Napoleon III's son; bakers and pastry-cooks with elaborate sculptures; saddlers and boot-makers, potters, stone-masons, coopers, carpenters and blacksmiths... There is an enamelled china drinking flask in the shape of a buoy, a seamless leather boot decorated with a mosaic of tiny pearls, complicated marquetry pieces and wrought-iron gates. Farriers are represented by an exquisite example of the traditional *bouquet de Saint Eloi*, the metal flower arrangement that was both a sign and a tribute to the patron saint of blacksmiths and metal-workers see (page 53).

## A revitalized contemporary scene

Not all crafts survived the upheavals and economic realities of the twentieth century. Those which did, and they are surprisingly many in France, still present a vigorous and variegated picture. With so rich a background of tradition, indviduality and protectionism, in most cases the vital link with the past has not been lost. There has been continuity – a new generation of potters taking over a family business, qualified dedicated newcomers revitalizing an authentic glassworks, young artisans passionately exploring old skills. In the last decade of the century, the spirit of the age, a rediscovered feeling for simplicity and well-made hand crafted objects has helped, but it is entirely to the artisans' credit that they took sound and often tough commercial decisions. This often involved opening their doors to visitors – not just the doors of their shops, but more importantly those of their workshops.

When I started my own modest *Tour de France* of country crafts to research this book, one thing I soon found out the successful contemporary artisans, the survivors, had in common was the uncompromising pursuit of quality. Some were quiet about it, others made a selling point of it ... but somehow it was always there

My travels started appropriately enough in Tours, in a restaurant called La Ciboulette just off the lively place Plumereau and its gabled buildings. Place Plumereau is in the old trading district where streets and squares have names like rue du Grand-Marché, place des Halles, rue de la Scellerie, place Foire-le-Roi, rue des Tanneurs and rue de la Monnaie. You have to be very dull of soul indeed not to be aware of a whiff of history. It was a hot summer's day in 1991 and an occasion I shall always cherish. The combined age of my two luncheon companions was one hundred and ninety. My grand-father (age 98) had been delighted to hear about the projected *French Country Crafts*. After sending me dozens of relevant addresses, magazine cuttings and articles, he had arranged for the two of us to have lunch with his old friend Roger Lecotté (age 92), '*pour tu puisses commencer tes recherches pour ton livre sur l'artisanat*' – for you to start researching your book on crafts... Monsieur Lecotté had been the inspiration behind the *Musée du Compagnonnage* and its Curator. He was a great and respected authority on crafts, folklore and *compagnonnage*.

Neither their age nor the day's heat had diminished my companions' wits or appetite. We had a delicious three-course meal and shared a bottle of cool young Gamay de Touraine. Notebook in hand, I listened to Monsieur Lecotté's reminiscences – often shrewdly prompted by my grandfather. Roger Lecotté's enthusiasm for his subject, for the handing-down and renewal of the best craft techniques and traditions was contagious. Every now and then Madame, the owner of the restaurant, came to check that everything was all right. Monsieur even left his kitchen to say hello. The fuss over my remarkable companions was quite proper and I felt they were enjoying it. Afterwards I found out that Monsieur Lecotté who lived on his own in a tiny flat next door to La Ciboulette was a very special customer indeed, one to whom the restaurant brought a light supper every night 'just in case he had nothing to eat'…

Monsieur Lecotté died a few months later of a sudden heart attack. As he once wrote of the joyful spirit of *compagnonnage*, '*la fête toujours devant un verre de vin*', what could be better than live as a moving feast always with a glass in hand? The enthusiasm he had communicated that afternoon in Tours stayed with me throughout my voyages around French crafts.

A craftsman varnishes a double-bass in Mirecourt, eastern France. Mirecourt, Lorraine, has traditionally been the centre of hand manufactured of stringed instruments in France.

A *jardinière* ready to leave the
decorating station. The dark blue
*Bleu de Giens* background is a great
classic of the Faïençerie.

# CERAMICS

Clay, water and wood… the essential ingredients of ceramics have always been plentiful in the large and varied expanses of the French countryside. The other important factor in the development of ceramics is a stable agrarian society – which did endure in France, albeit with some hiccups, until well into this century.

Along with other traditional crafts, ceramics suffered after the First World War. The surviving soldiers returned to changing villages which their descendants, in their turn, were in a hurry to abandon. The demand for everyday clay utensils and containers dwindled miserably, particularly with the advent of plastic and the increased domestic use of refrigerators.

This depressed state of affairs reached an all-time low in the early Sixties. Thereafter, however, a more affluent society, combined with a change in values and priorities and a yearning for the quality and simplicity of the uncluttered old rural lifestyle, have gradually given French ceramics a fresh lease of life.

New potters have started to work at the wheel – many of them 'drop-outs' from the urban 'rat race' after the inconclusive events of 1968. All have had to work hard at their marketing skills, as the demand for hand-crafted pots and dishes is no longer automatic. Unlike the old-fashioned customers, the new clients are at least as interested in the visual as the practical.

For the interested would-be buyer, French country ceramics – from the humblest pottery to the most sophisticated *faïenceries* – offer great bargains and a wealth of finds.

## THE FAÏENCERIE AT GIEN

The factories of the Faïencerie at Gien on the Loire bring traditional rural skills to the luxury goods end of light industry in a most impressive manner. The old and the new are smoothly combined in elegant classical buildings which house state-of-the-art plant, allowing modern production techniques and sophisticated marketing to capitalize on good old-fashioned perfectionist know-how.

Gien faience is made from a very fine white paste – a combination of

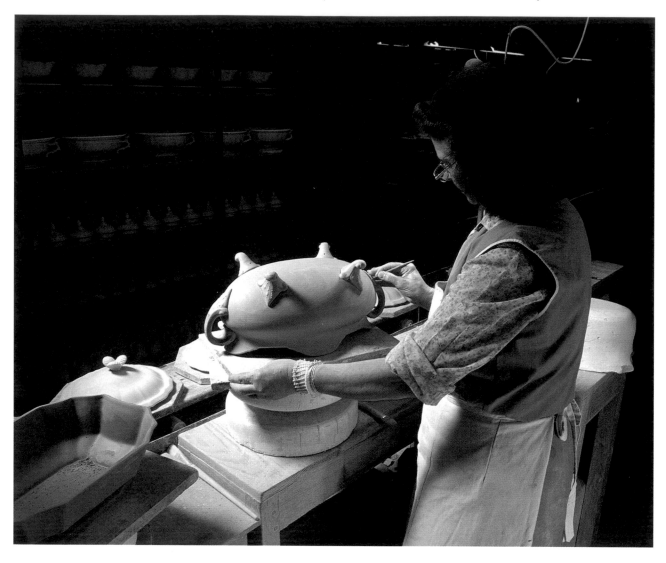

Still an anonymous plain *biscuit* at this stage, the *jardinière* is fitted with legs.

kaolin, clay and sand – which is poured into a mould or pressed between two moulds. Thus formed, it is dried then polished and later fired to make the 'biscuit'. So far, so good. The part of the Faïencerie which carries out this manufacturing process seemed huge and mechanized after the crowded small workshops we had visited. It was also spotlessly clean, as impeccable as a medical research laboratory.

Much more interesting and relevant for our purposes were the workshops involved in the decoration of the faience. Here the 'biscuit' vase, plate or flower stand is transformed into an object that is unmistakably Gien. Not surprisingly, this is also the stage at which the piece of china becomes valuable. Biscuit is cheap to produce and fairly large stocks of it are kept. The expensive, time-consuming and labour-intensive process of decoration then tends to take place to order.

Like the feet, the handles are attached with *barbotine*, the clay and water paste that is used as a standard adhesive.

A number of traditional techniques are used at Gien to transfer motifs to the biscuit, including copperplate engraving by hand, stencils and silk-screens. Chromolithography is also used on some enamelled china.

Many pieces are hand-painted, the artisan minutely brushing colour within the outline. The paint station – and the area of the works which seemed to enjoy the best natural light – was a fascinating place at which to linger. A row of white desks faced long windows, looking out on a peaceful inner courtyard. The painters were all women, quietly absorbed in their work, with brushes and pots neatly arranged at hand, colour pattern not far away. Only a fat pet cat was allowed to disrupt their concentration. It takes an experienced artisan a day's work to paint a jardinière (the flower or plant stand so beloved of the bourgeoisie around the turn of the century).

Some areas, like handles which are stuck on with *barbotine*, have to be

The decorative design is first outlined (*right*), then the pieces are painted by hand (*below*).

## HOW FAIENCE CAME TO GIEN

The enamelled clay pottery that is known as faience is named after the Italian town of Faenza, home of ceramics works renowned throughout Europe since the early Renaissance. In the Baroque era at the end of the sixteenth century, Faenza perfected a white enamel which set off the painted motifs. Deep dark blues, yellows and muted orange were favourite colours. Faenza-trained Italian artisans began to travel around Europe, teaching their skills and setting up workshops. In France they settled in Nîmes, Nevers, Rouen, Moutiers, Lyons and Montpellier.

Business really took off at the end of the seventeenth century, when Louis XIV had his gold and silver tableware melted down in order to fund his latest set of ruinous military campaigns. As usual, courtiers were not tardy in following their monarch's example and faience plates soon began to replace silver on the tables of the aristocracy.

French *faïenceries* were subsequently badly hit by the Revolution and by competition from Britain, with the production of fine china in Staffordshire. The factory at Gien was, in fact, started in 1821 by an enterprising Englishman, Thomas Hall, who decided it would be easier to manufacture in France than to import from England. Gien struck him as a perfect location to set up a fine china works *à l'anglaise*, as the conditions were ideal: clay, sand and siliceous stones from the Loire and plenty of wood to the north in the forests around Orleans.

painted without outlines. Even more skilled, this task is the responsibility of a couple of specialists. Very few people can be trusted to paint free-hand – particularly when the precious object they happen to be painting already represents hours and hours of expert work.

Decorated pieces are then enamelled: first they are plunged into a milky bath – not of asses' milk, although it did look silky-soft and performed wonders for the texture of the china; it is in fact a fine ground-glass emulsion. Returned to the kiln at around 1,080°C (2,000°F), the finished faience then emerges in all its beauty, brought to gleaming or satin-like life by the fire.

Is there such a thing as a Gien look? Is there a sure way of telling that a piece of china comes from Gien? It will, of course, bear the distinctive discreet stamped motif of three chimneys. The visitor to the Musée de la Faïencerie de Gien and to its shop will, however, be dazed by the rich variety of patterns and colours. Unlike Delft, for instance, Gien faience has many looks. There is, of course, the famed intense *Bleu de Gien*, with that midnight-blue background which goes straight back to the Italian Renaissance. However, there is a myriad of other designs, classics that never go out of fashion: a discreet cashmere pattern has been popular since the last century, as have more flamboyant peonies and peacocks. From the eighteenth century comes the elegant bird of paradise, and there is also a little bluebird chirping irresistibly on a naive folk-art blue background.

Since owners Pierre and Evelyne Jeufroy took over the factory in 1984, artists and designers have worked with the *faïencerie* to create a new generation of patterns. Such well-known names as Paco Rabanne, Andrée Putnam, Garouste & Bonetti, Eliakim, Bill Goldsmith and Dominique Lalande have produced designs which are very modern, not to say avant garde. All have been turned into faultless faience and will help take Gien into the next century.

## THE SALT-GLAZED POTS OF NORON

Stony of heart is the visitor who has never succumbed to the charm of a French place name, never made a meandering detour to see whether X-ville-sous-Bois, Sainte-X-la-Jolie or Quelquechose-les-Vignes lived up to its tag. If you happen to be intrigued by the description and not in a hurry, it is a rewarding way to travel. Some forays, of course, are happier than others.

In the quest for traditional crafts, going by place names can be a hit-and-miss business. A specialist skill or trade may still be part of a locality's name even though it is, alas, long since dead. The twentieth century has been harsh to old villages: many of them have gradually lost their *raison d'être*, their main business dwindling away until they have virtually become ghost towns.

I remember making one such lure-of-the-place-name detour in order to drive through Saint-Jean-la-Poterie in southern Brittany. It was late on a tormented grey afternoon, full of wind and rain and with the odd luminous break in the clouds. I was prepared for a melancholy scene, perhaps a run-down workshop, dusty imported clay knick-knacks in the gift corner of the Arts et Presse store, abandoned grass-covered kilns in backyards. What I found was a quiet empty place with no sign whatsoever of pottery-related activity. Not a kiln, not a *poterie*, not even a tourist trap of a souvenir shop. A small café did call itself Le Bar de la Faïencerie, but there was no sign of any factory.

Back in Paris I consulted the archives in the library of the Musée des Arts et Traditions Populaires. Saint-Jean-la-Poterie has its own thick file which made sad reading. The village had been a well-known craft centre and the object of a detailed lengthy study. Of the dozens of potters active – if perhaps not thriving – at the beginning of the century, only a few were left after the last war. Fewer still survived at the beginning of the Sixties, when the research ended.

The case-story was illustrated with photographs – some sepia and very old, others post-war, square and sharply focused – all very moving. These showed kiln after kiln, displays of no-nonsense pots and plates destined for everyday practical use, and generations of strong-faced potters, male and female, intent on their work (see page 8). And then there were none! Where were all the potters gone?

Closing the file, I recalled the village I had driven through. The kilns had been replaced by neat villas and, judging by the cars and *soigné* gardens, the potters had been usurped by prosperous commuters.

My next stop at a -la-Poterie village was a much more propitious occasion, very well worth the detour, in fact. Noron-la-Poterie in Normandy is easy to find, just off the main road between Bayeux and Saint-Lô, a dozen kilometres from Bayeux. Like Saint-Jean, Noron has a bulging folder in the reference library of the Musée des Arts et Traditions Populaires. It has been a pottery centre for centuries, thanks to the local clay, the good *terre de Noron* dug up 4-metres (13 feet) deep, which produces distinctively brown pottery with rich auburn overtones. Although gas is used nowadays, in the old days the kilns were fired with wood, and there are still plenty of trees in the area where once stood a huge birch forest.

Every pottery centre has its own look and speciality. Like Saint Amand la Pusaye in Burgundy and a few centres such as Betschdorf in the Alsace, Noron traditionally uses salt to glaze the fired biscuit. Liberal handfuls of coarse salt are thrown into the kiln late in the firing process. The fumes create a shiny glass-like finish which is tough enough to obviate the need for enamelling. As in Saint Amand, the clay mined locally can cope with very high temperatures and salt glazing takes place at around 1,200°C (2,200°F).

Both clay and salt are food- and beverage-friendly materials. Perhaps as a

Jars and flower pots in the yard outside the Dubosts' pottery in Noron.

Assorted jugs and pitchers with a
gently rounded shape that has
remained unchanged for centuries.

A jug gradually emerging on the
potter's wheel.

Gathering clay dust on a window-sill, forgotten pots bask in the sunlight.

Miniature Calvados jugs (*above and far right*) are decorated with the popular fruit and leaf motif before they are fired.

result of this, Noron produces unpretentious everyday containers, the kind of pots, jars, bowls and basins that have been used for storing food throughout the ages. Not surprisingly in the heart of Normandy – the land of dairy products – there are lots of milk jugs, bowls, vats and moulds for making cheese and butter.

This is also apple and Calvados country. *Noblesse oblige*, the most famous of the Noron products is the *cruchon à calva*, the rounded pitcher decorated with apples, grapes and leaves that is so much part of the local scene. Scholarly purists frown on the calva pitcher, with its stuck-on *décor*, as a vulgar late-nineteenth century commercial ploy. Provided that they are large enough, however, they can be very attractive. The miniature versions do look a little absurd – but so do mini-vats, moulds and jugs. Rustic pottery is nothing if not practical and there is a rightness about the original size of day-to-day traditional clay utensils which vanishes once the objects are scaled down – their simple beauty evaporating as they dwindle into mere knick-knacks.

Noron became famous in the eighteenth and nineteenth centuries. It supplied the farmers of Normandy, Brittany and the Maine with their butter

*Opposite* Square flower pots are always in demand. More intriguing is the half-pan used for baking apples on the outside of the hearth (*below*). The squat jug (*right*) was traditionally used to keep water hot in the baker's oven and the plump pot with a lid (*below right*) for storing pork fat.

and cream vats, their jars for storing pork fat, their cider jugs and their coffee pots. Madame Dubost, who with her husband Jean owns and runs the main pottery of the village, had a rather alarming story to relate about the tall straight *cane à café* coffee pot. Coffee used to be made once a week and reheated as necessary. No wonder liberal amounts of calva were used to dose the brew to make it palatable.

If Noron survives on the pottery map of France, it is largely thanks to the commitment and hard work of Monsieur and Madame Dubost. They fell in love with the village during a chance visit and bought the *poterie* in 1966 from an old master potter. Jean Guitton had been working the pottery since its heyday in 1925, when it employed thirty-five people and when many houses in Noron still had their own kiln and workshop. Monsieur Guitton was a potter of the old school, who passed on his knowledge and expertise to the new owners… just in time! By the mid-Sixties, in the brave new modern France of General de Gaulle, refrigerators and plastic containers had made the old clay utensils practically obsolete. Demand for pots was diminishing as fast as the traditional rural clientele was moving to cities and factories.

Over the years, with many ups and downs, the Dubosts have concentrated on adapting production and marketing to the changing times. Equipment has been modernized and new kilns installed, but traditional clay working and turning techniques have been maintained and the more decorative of the old lines are still in production. They are still practical unpretentious everyday objects. However, the Dubosts also want their products to appeal to people for aesthetic reasons. As a result new colours have been added, including a discreet palish beige and a strong metallic blue.

It is only too easy to linger in the pottery shop. The warm brown salt-glazed clays of Noron, with their rounded shapes, look warm and inviting – sometimes mysteriously so. I had often wondered why so many old clay bottles had two flattened sides: 'so that they don't roll about when you put them in carts to bring cider or wine to the workers in the fields,' said Madame Dubost. The mystery is solved, but the sight of my no-longer strange bottle gives me just as much pleasure even now that I know the story behind it.

## THE ANCIENT CLAY POTTERY
## OF CLIOUSCLAT

The Autoroute du Soleil – or, more prosaically, the A7 – is a tantalizing road. One temptation is to put on your blinkers, ignore the scenery and speed down to Provence, smart Europe's favourite holiday or retirement destination. Ah, the lure of the sun, the light, the cicadas and the sweet smells of herbs… The other option, particularly if you have been to Provence before and are past

Orchards in blossom near Cliousclat in the Rhône Valley.

your teens or early twenties, is to succumb to the call of the landscape and to branch out to discover what the big country has to offer.

With every mile that passes as you drive south of Tain l'Ermitage, this lure becomes harder and harder to resist. Especially as the southern Rhône valley is a land of contrasts: relentless winds, extreme heat, abandoned-looking stone hamlets, mile after mile of luxuriant orchards and the occasional gem of a village, building or craft centre.

I am going to give lovers of pottery a trip worth the detour. Allowing

After a spring shower the yard of the pottery takes on a fresh but melancholy look.

several hours (for there is a delicious simple local restaurant as well as splendid pottery), abandon the motorway after Valence and drive through Loriol. Take small roads south towards Montélimar and, perhaps after a wrong turn or two because the sign-posting is somewhat scanty, you will find the village of Cliousclat. Here, varnished clay pottery has been made since the tenth century and probably much earlier.

Cliousclat is minuscule and pampered, without being in any way tarted up. It consists of only two or three very narrow streets made up of well-kept houses built of cream-coloured stone with plenty of flowers on windowsills and doorsteps.

I was last there in the spring, and everywhere I looked peach blossoms were fluttering in the distance in the gaps between the houses. It was a day of intermittent showers, and the courtyard of the pottery – which is reached through an unusual covered passage you cannot miss as you walk around the tiny village – had a melancholy, untidy aspect. In fine weather pots are allowed to dry outside on long planks skilfully laid across tree trunks, but only a few finished garden pots were out that day.

The pottery itself is a long, low-ceilinged building, on the left. Underneath is the cellar where the clay loaves are kept, the shop is on the right and another building shelters the yard – and the drying pots – from the north wind. What looked like an embryo bower was in the process of being built.

I knocked on the door of the workshop, but there was no reply. The shop was open, but unattended. Very trusting people, I thought, looking at rows of finely decorated gleaming bowls and platters. My watch said 12.45. I should have known better: lunchtime is not a good time to arrive note-pad and pencil in hand anywhere in France.

I was on the point of retreating until two, better still two-thirty, to allow my subjects a little *siesta* time, when a powerful smell of charred lamb and rosemary hit my nostrils and led me by the nose through the courtyard. The owners of the pottery, Nicolas and Olivier Sourdive, were *à table*, enjoying lunch with their families, friends and employees. A dozen happy faces, some a little clay-splattered, beamed at me.

Nicolas Sourdive got up from the upturned bucket on which he was sitting, shook my hand and explained that they were celebrating the visit of a former *compagnon*. He directed me to the village restaurant – where I too had lamb, fragrantly casseroled with lots of herbs, and admired more of the Sourdives' output, displayed without pretension. The restaurant was clearly the local canteen and meeting place, and Nicolas later joined me there for coffee.

Was the *compagnon* they were celebrating a member of the association, doing his *Tour de France du Compagnonnage*, gathering experience and know-how from master-craftsmen as he travelled around the country? I was hoping for a positive answer, but Nicolas told me that he was instead an independent potter. The word *compagnon* has always been part of the craftsman's vocabu-

A cyclamen creates a splash of colour in a plain clay urn … Pottery containers enable Provençal villages to flower without using up precious water supplies.

The drying pots are carefully balanced on wooden planks and moved along to make room for new additions.

lary. It tends to be used to describe someone no longer an apprentice, but in temporary employment. In other walks of life and modern parlance, the phrase might be 'on secondment'. Commercial French has a word for it, *stagiaire*, which is definitely not as evocative.

The *poterie* run by the Sourdive brothers was the brainchild of a local potter, Marius Anjaleras, who designed and built it at the beginning of the century. Marius had everything well planned. First he borrowed money to build the wood-fired kiln still found there and described by Nicolas as 'the heart and soul of the place' and was thus able to start work virtually at once. After a few years in production he was able to buy the brick vats where the clay is stored and decanted after being plunged in water. Then came the purchase of the land from which the raw clay is extracted.

The clay around Cliousclat is very pale, practically white, and remarkably neutral. *'Elle ne donne pas de goût'* (it leaves no taste), which gives the potters plenty of scope for achieving the delicately coloured glazes that are

Throwing the bigger pots requires skill and strength and is only entrusted to experienced potters.

Engrossed in their work: a young potter finishes off a small *jardinière* (*left*), young Manon Sourdive learns the family craft (*below*) while her father decorates a bowl with light brush strokes and a practised hand (*opposite*).

characteristic of the Cliousclat pots, particularly the lovely gentle, creamy-yellow which often acts as a background for the *décor*.

The decoration is a tradition reborn. Throughout the ages, artisans have used decoration as an expression of their skills and personalities, to transform practical everyday objects into something closer to a work of art. Some motifs were traditional or ritual, others were created to celebrate an occasion such as a wedding, birth or anniversary. In Cliousclat, this dedicated *décor* could perhaps be a woman with a bird and dog drawn with a light brush on a platter intended as a fiftieth birthday present and inscribed for the lady for whom it was destined. Following the potter's inspiration, *décors* are delicately etched or brushed, or sometimes dribbled to give a soft, mottled effect.

As was the case in not-so-distant Dieulefit, some 60 kilometres (35 miles) to the south-east, throughout the centuries pots and platters in Cliousclat were always intended as containers for foodstuffs. They were made to keep milk, olive oil or wine, to preserve fats, jams and charcuterie; for use in making cheeses and candied fruit, for storing chestnuts, olives and grains. As in the rest of the region and also in the heart of Provence, tableware was usually a ceramic glazed with a lead mixture. In Cliousclat this varnish is made of lead ore mixed with ground sand and Bresse earth. Yet another legacy from the days of the Moors, those great trail-blazers in the field of ceramics, this distinctive finish is known as *alquifoux*, a straight translation from Arabic *al-kuhul*, via the Spanish *alquifu*, a lead varnish.

Monsieur Anjaleras started the works at what was to be a critical and sad time in the history of pottery. In the golden days of the nineteenth century, every house in Cliousclat had its wheel and the village boasted several kilns. One by one they disappeared as the young people of the village left to seek pastures new *à l'étranger*, perhaps in Marseilles or Lyons.

In 1964 Nicolas's and Olivier's father, Philippe Sourdive, bought the pottery from the Anjaleras family. Trained as a ceramicist, Monsieur Sourdive had a passion for rescuing from oblivion 'beautiful objects which should not die'. In museums in Marseilles and Strasbourg, in old attics, in cellars and corners of neglected houses in the region, he looked for traditional Cliousclat pottery.

He was particularly interested in the *décor*, added 'by the human hand' using fine lines of reddish brown, green or black. Decoration had not been a priority with the previous owners. Struggling as they were against the times, they had wisely concentrated on diversifying into areas such as rounded garden pots and big pieces, and novelty goods – known locally as *censibelle* or *bricole*, including tiny coffee cups and the charming *rossignol* or nightingale, a little water jug which sings when you fill it with water.

The Sourdive brothers have kept up their father's work. In the shop the shelves display fine, large bowls, deep dishes and platters gleaming like runny honey. The *décor* motifs are very nicely balanced between recherché and

Less fragile pots are stored outside in the sheltered yard of the pottery.

Differently decorated bowls before and after the firing which allows their brilliance to shine through.

naive, elegant folk art but not 'art'. The present generation of Sourdives seems to work well as a team, amiably sharing the job of running the pottery. Olivier concentrates on the marketing and Nicolas on the pots themselves.

He runs a relaxed but purposeful workshop. On the day we visited to take the photographs, a potter throwing large urns and a young woman doing smaller pieces occasionally had to slalom between our lights and tripods in order to lift planks of drying pots and move them up the drying rota. They concentrated on their work, as totally unperturbed by the clicking of the camera as by the comings and goings of various visitors in rain-soaked clothes discussing the progress of the bower construction. The only person who took any notice was little Manon, well wrapped up and home from school with tonsillitis, proudly showing her father Nicolas the rather abstract clay shapes she was making.

He coped ably with her and with my questions while continuing to hand-decorate shallow bowls that my covetous eye thought would make splendid salad dishes. Bowl after bowl gently turned, and as the hand lightly moved, there emerged fresh flowery patterns all just a little different. It all seemed deceptively effortless. 'Well it is, after a while,' said Nicolas. 'but wait until you see it come alive with firing, all the pigments in the slip coming to life…'

## SALERNES – CAPITAL OF TILES

The French love their capitals of this and that, and various towns fight very hard for the coveted title of *La Capitale de Quelquechose…* whether it be lace, *boudin*, candied violets or copper. The little town of Salernes in the rugged hills of the Var, 25 kilometres (15 miles) west of Draguignan, is no exception. Its claim to fame is that it is *La Capitale du Carrelage*, the capital of traditional floor and wall tiles. Its most sought-after and celebrated product is the *tomette*, a hard-wearing hexagonal red clay tile that has never gone out of fashion.

Salernes, or rather the site that was to become Salernes, has been involved in ceramics for thousands of years, arguably for much longer than most places in western Europe. Remains found in the area have been traced back to 5000 BC. Vast pits of red clay, rich in iron and eminently suitable for firing, were deposited there during the Tertiary geological era. Production was at first solely for local use, but ever since the Renaissance an abundance of workshops and factories has meant that the tiles of Salernes graced grand and bourgeois floors in Marseilles, Lyons, Avignon – and even across the Mediterranean in North Africa.

Production started to decline with the First World War – a familiar enough

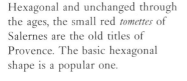

Hexagonal and unchanged through the ages, the small red *tomettes* of Salernes are the old titles of Provence. The basic hexagonal shape is a popular one.

story – and did not pick up in the following decades. Demand was badly hit by cheap imports, the fashion for cement quarry tiles and the advent of plastic and other synthetics. It was, however, a case of losing a battle not the war.

Visitors to Salernes will not fail to notice the number of businesses specializing in floor and wall coverings. The roads in and out of the town are crammed with billboards and signs advertising tiles – *tomettes* and *carrelages* – not necessarily to the greater beauty of the immediate environment. The tide of fashion has turned and people are now prepared to pay a little more for something authentic that looks hand-made and has a strong regional feel.

Salernes is in the heart of a still-unspoilt but fast-developing part of Provence, a popular holiday home choice for the French and francophile

A new look for a traditional local craft. Well situated an hour's drive away from the crowded Mediterranean coast, the old tile capital of Salernes has remained a busy place. Young market-conscious artisans have attracted new customers for whom the design of everyday objects matters at least as much as their functional aspect.

*étrangers* – particularly, it appears, the English and the Dutch. Local tiles are as apt a choice for the new residents as they have always been for the old. If you do not have the good fortune to own a little house somewhere in the hills, you can always take home a carload of *tomettes* for your suburban patio.

The visitor to Salernes is well advised not to give up in despair at the sight of the forest of signs. The little streets of the old town have a great deal of charm and much to offer. I had a happy time in an untidy shop called 'La Grange', run by an artist potter's wife with contagious enthusiasm for the decorated ceramics which she was selling. Her shop also seemed to be a habitual meeting place for the inhabitants of Salernes – the sort of place where you are welcome to wait for your bus on a wet day.

If what you are after is traditional *tomettes* or plain terracotta floor tiles, a good place to visit is J. Sismondini, a few miles outside Salernes on the windy Sillans-la-Cascade road. In addition to the *specialité du pays*, the inevitable *tomette*, they make tiles in several shapes and sizes: square, octagonal, rectangular, etc. The tiles are baked in a traditional wood-fired kiln and individually checked for quality. The colours on offer also vary, but all have the typical red iron hue of the region.

While the Sismondini family, a long-established local dynasty, has remained in the business of producing traditional tiles, others have diversified into enamelled tiles and a whole range of colours and patterns with a more decorative function. For example, Alain Vagh has been on the Draguignan road in Salernes since the late Sixties. Bringing home a bootful of his lovely tiles was sadly out of the question financially, but starting a few-at-a-time collection proved irresistible.

Bunches of grapes embossed on tiles.

## LA POTERIE PROVENÇALE IN BIOT

Just outside Biot, going down towards the sea, on the left behind two wide rusty gates you will suddenly see rows and rows of big jars in a large courtyard. You are at La Poterie Provençale, famed for its extraordinary range of garden vases and for its boldly coloured tableware.

Of the hundreds of jars and urns competing to catch someone's eye outside the pottery, no two are quite the same. The big pots come in dozens of shapes,

Robust uncompromising shapes and colours are typical of the Poterie Provençale's output. The distinct green (*below*) of the tableware is as strong as the simplicity of the plain garden urns.

Rows and rows of jars, all with a marked family resemblance but each slightly different ... Genuine Poterie Provençale pieces are stamped with the double eight hallmark (*below*). Legend has it that the town of Biot was founded by two Genoese families, each with eight members, *bi-otto*.

some plump enough to provide a comfortable hiding-place for the fattest of Ali Baba's forty thieves, while others are incredibly svelte and tall. All say, 'Touch me!' Most are plain, but a few are ornamented with a stuck-on motif, such as a lion's head, a rope or a flower. Colours are a variation on a theme of beige, with a hint of pink, a coral blush, a touch of yellow, a sunburnt look or a pale creamy complexion. The finish is a smooth matt, although rims are sometimes coated with a darker varnish which is allowed to dribble a little way down the sides. Often the pots are left completely unadorned.

In true Provençal fashion – and also because the urns are for the garden – the courtyard acts as principal stockroom and showroom. On the left as you walk in are gathered the pots on order waiting to be collected. Displayed a touch less casually across the way are the pots for sale. It is easy to spend a good half-hour wandering around, savouring the various shapes from different angles and enjoying the way the light and shadows fall on them.

With its casual displays of tempting tableware, its potted plants and old furniture, the showroom has a timeless air.

You will be greeted on arrival by the pottery staff, but otherwise left in peace – hard selling is not the style of La Poterie Provençale. Dotted around the pots on display are a number of venerable senior urns – a little weather-worn – which clearly will never leave the pottery. If you are there at the right time of the year, they may contain a camellia or magnolia plant in full blossom or even a citrus tree in fruit.

The showroom proper, with big windows rather like a conservatory, has a gently faded look. Dust hangs in the air and falls on the displayed plates, bowls and dishes. The tableware is green, blue, white, a beautiful intense black, pale or dark yellow. The owner, Monsieur Augé-Laribé, informs us that green is the best selling colour. I like the green – somewhere in between spinach and olive, bright without being garish, it is a shade that will make most food look appetizing and is wonderful on a white tablecloth. Somehow it seems familiar... I am sure I have admired it before.

Monsieur Augé-Laribé gently carries on with his explanations. If green has become so successful, it is because the English have started a trend. The English? Does La Poterie have representatives in England? No, no reps, never. People come to us, says the owner with an element of quiet pride. It turns out that I have seen La Poterie Provençale's green tableware in one of my

favourite local cookware shops, The French Kitchen shop in London's Westbourne Grove. *Quelle coïncidence, ça par example...*

Monsieur Augé-Laribé confides that, with a small staff, his real problem is meeting orders, not finding customers. He feels that the current French government is making life unnecessarily hard for small businesses with high taxes and employers' contributions. It is a story that I have heard time and time again in my discussions with French artisans. Many prefer to work on their own rather than go through the administrative complications and high hidden costs of employing people to help them.

After the brightness of the courtyard and the airy light of the showroom, walking into the shop is like stepping inside a giant walk-in cupboard. It is cool and dark, with shelves and shelves of assorted plates, dishes, bowls, platters, jugs, cups and saucers – perfect for some lucky bride. Most are stacked up in piles, but some are displayed upright.

I particularly liked the soup tureens on the central table. Classic and comforting, with their matching hollow plates, all satisfactorily just a little uneven, this is the hand-finish of *artisanat*, not the uniformity of industrial machinery. Monsieur Augé-Laribé shows me the stamp guaranteeing quality and origin and explains that the little notches sometimes seen on the bottom rim of plates are made by the points on which the plates rest during firing.

Also tempting are the table fountains, Provence's answer to samovars, which were used to hold drinking water. You turned on the little tap and a cool trickle came out. If I am writing this in the past tense, it is because the Poterie's *fontaines* reminded me of blissfully messy childhood games with a similar container in my grandparents' dining-room.

Monsieur Augé-Laribé takes us backstage. We are going to see the pottery in stages of production. Behind the main buildings we walk through a shed piled high with several heaps of clay of different colours – pale, grey and reddish – into a large backyard. In it are pools filled with parched earth, some with weeds sprouting through the crevices. This is the decanted drying clay, almost ready to be cut up into blocks for further refining. Drying takes a matter of days in summer under the fierce sun but is, of course, a great deal slower in winter.

The clay used at the pottery no longer comes from local quarries, but much is still extracted in the *département*, the Alpes-Maritimes. Some is brought from as far as Seine-et-Marne in northern France – La Poterie Provençale's 'mix' of clays is a complex and unique cocktail. Since this is a secret recipe that I am unlikely ever to understand, let alone try to emulate, I am happy to move on to the workshop.

Here is where the big jars are made. Even my untrained eye can see that this is a genuine photographer's delight: the soil of rough beaten earth and the beige dust dancing in the air, the light streaming in from the windows playing on the strange shapes of gauges and template frames hanging on the walls, the

A view of the main workshop, with the sunlight streaming around rows of drying jars.

Coils of rope and potter's wheels
waiting to be used.

Drying jars still with the coils of
rope on to which the potter slapped
the clay. Only when the jars are
completely dry will he remove the
ropes which hold them together.

well-worn tools, the drying jars still with their rough, uneven rims, many containing what appeared to be coils of rope.

The reason for the ropes is simple. Very large jars are made on a low potter's wheel, with a square axle in the centre, set in a depression in the ground. Slats of wood are placed at intervals around the wheel and surrounded with rope. The potter then slaps the clay on to the rope until the layer of clay is thick enough to rub against the gauge or fixed external mould. The slats of wood are then carefully taken out and the jar, still supported by the coil of rope, is left to dry for a few days. The cord is then removed and, hey presto, the jar is polished and the rim finished.

When the jar is particularly tall and thin, with a rim that is narrower than the base, it is made upside down and the base stuck on later with *barbotine*, the mixture of clay and water that is commonly used for decorating pots and which acts as an all-purpose glue.

The skilled business of throwing a tall jar requires a good hour-and-a-half and the the efforts of two potters – hence the hole in the ground to make the top of the jar easier to work. The tallest of the Biot jars measure up to 1.3 metres in height (well over 4 feet). Their elegance is deceptive – for all their slenderness, they weigh a very solid hundred or so kilos (about 2 hundredweight).

Monsieur Augé-Laribé reckons that most people can become useful potters in a year or so. Mastering the use of the rope and throwing the large jars, however, puts you altogether in a different league and not everybody can do it. He modestly admits that, unlike his father and now his own son, he does not 'throw' himself. Decorating the pots, yes, running the business, definitely, but the *tour à corde*, the wheel with the rope, no!

After the pots have dried, which can take several weeks if they are very large, there comes the firing, literally a make-or-break operation. Filling the kiln takes a week of careful arranging and shelving: large pots in the bottom, smaller pots inside bigger pots, not a centimetre of space wasted. The oil-fired kiln is gradually brought up to a temperature of around 950°C (1,750°F) and the pots are cooked for two days. They are then left to cool very slowly in the kiln over a week – an abrupt change of temperature would cause them to crack. *Toute une production*, a real performance, my host readily admits.

# METALWORK AND JEWELLERY

Legend has it that Saint Eloi, patron saint of French metalworkers – from goldsmiths to blacksmiths – was nothing if not resourceful. One day, exasperated by a frisky horse, he simply cut off one of its front legs, shoed the hoof in peace, then stuck the leg back on. In another well-loved episode from his busy life, he got the better of the Devil masquerading as a naughty temptress. Ignoring the advances that were being made to him, the good smith and bishop just caught the Devil's nose between red-hot pincers.

Faced with a changing world, many of the metal craftsmen have managed to display a resourcefulness worthy of their patron. They have opened their workshops to the public to make visitors aware of the skilled labour that goes into the finished crafted objects, whether they are knives or copper kettles. They have also learned to diversify into new areas of expertise, from agricultural tools to fine wrought-iron creations.

If Saint Eloi is still watching over his protégés from the great forge in the sky, he will find much of which to be proud.

## COPPER CITY

Few French towns are able to boast as intriguing a name as Villedieu-les-Poêles – the 'Town of God and of Frying Pans'. The juxtaposition of the divine and the homely sounds more bizarre still in literal translation. Yet some very light delving into local history soon shows that it was the presence of the former which helped the latter to prosper.

Once upon a time, around AD 1130 to be precise, the Order of Saint John of Jerusalem – precursor to the Knights of Malta – was granted land in Normandy by Henry I, son of William the Conqueror and King of England. Thirty kilometres (19 miles) from the sea, not far from Mont Saint Michel, the order built a foundation in their new territory, a House of God, 'Maison-Dieu' in French, 'Villa Dei' in Latin. The site soon became known as Villedieu.

Rhythmically wielding his hammer, a craftsman beats a preserving pan until it is smooth and shiny.

The tools of the coppersmith's trade have changed little over the centuries. It takes a craftsman thousand of hammer blows and hours of work to hand craft a preserving pan.

The Knights of Malta's allegiance was to the Pope, not to the local king or bishop. One of the perks resulting from this was that the land they controlled was exempt from the many taxes levied on medieval communities by the local powers that were. Despite the efforts of successive French kings and thanks to Villedieu's machiavellian negotiations, the city managed to remain a tax-free haven for several centuries – the last of its privileges being abolished only at the time of the Revolution.

With no hearth-tax, no mining tax, no toll and no mint tax to pay, but with a privileged location on the river Sienne at a busy crossroads, Villedieu soon prospered into a thriving commercial centre. Tanners and tawers plied their trade down by the river, but coppersmiths gradually outnumbered them. They made religious utensils, fittings for furniture and – increasingly – copper pans, *les poêles*. Thus Villedieu became Villedieu-les-Poêles.

Every household had to have a pan, and demand for this essential utensil remained steady for centuries. As early as 1329 the *poêliers* or pan-makers became organized into a trade association and built up a structure of complex statutes regulating social issues such as sickness benefits and dowries.

In Villedieu the steady rhythm of hammers hitting sheets of copper was heard everywhere. Traditional practices have remained the same for centuries. I was told that a skilled copper artisan hammers a piece once a second, some 3,600 times every hour-and-a-quarter (including the odd minute of rest). Newcomers to workshops take about three days to get used to the noise.

*Opposite* A main view of the old copper workshop.

In fact, deafness was an occupational hazard and the inhabitants of Villedieu were teased for their poor hearing: their old nickname of *les Sourdins*, 'the deaf ones', has stuck.

There were workshops all over the town, practically in every courtyard. To this day, the back streets bear tell-tale traces of centuries of metal-working. Wander into any little alleyway and everywhere you will see granite water troughs under old gutters and mysterious markings: deep notches on windowsills, angular stones polished smooth with use, steps worn by the nails of clogs, vertical scorings on the jamb of a gate-post where paring irons were once sharpened.

In the old days, the making of a pan always started in the communal furnace where regulations required the artisans to melt the metal they needed and to pay a levy that went to the coffers of their association. Needless to say, not everyone complied and there were always one or two hidden furnaces carrying on illegally. The old official furnace is now the site of a municipal museum, with a large collection of ancient copper utensils.

Today's Villedieu not only lives up to its old name-tag, but also probably off it. Pans have remained big business and if Villedieu is still on the map it is because of its traditional craft. The chances are that the first thing to catch your eye as you drive into town will be a copper pot gleaming to your left or to your right. Saucepans, vases, ashtrays, candlesticks, fish kettles, pitchers, key rings, fireguards, churns, warming pans ... copper is everywhere. Copper utensils line the main streets of the small town; they crowd shop windows; they hang in doorways; they are arranged on the pavement, shining on and off in the changing light.

And the light does change constantly. In that part of Normandy there is a saying *il fait beau vingt fois par jour* (it's a nice day twenty times a day). When I last visited, this was an understatement: sudden bouts of bright sunshine were constantly being replaced by fierce quick showers, making the copper look brilliant or dull by turns in a matter of minutes.

There is a danger that so much polished copper could look cloying and make Villedieu into a huge souvenir shop. Fortunately this is not the case, however, even to the critical eye of someone who is not particularly enamoured of artifacts made of copper. The town has remained handsome and robustly real. It is always lively and has a big market on Tuesdays. In fact, with its fine church, spacious main square, old houses and intriguing side streets, and with not a little help from the quirky sunlight, Villedieu carries off its copper displays with great charm.

The quality and the prices of the copper utensils and ornaments on show in the town vary enormously. Not surprisingly, the pieces that have been imported tend to be a lot cheaper. If you look at them closely and if you handle them, you will see that they tend to be lighter and less well-finished than those more expensive items which have been locally crafted and

The streets of Villedieu-les-Poêles have a friendly comfortable quality typical of Normandy.

hallmarked. Copper utensils are expensive and a clear case of getting what you pay for.

Whether or not you are prepared to pay for the difference may well depend on whether or not you take the time to visit l'Atelier du Cuivre. Located practically across the road from the old museum, l'Atelier is an active traditional copper workshop which also encourages the public to visit. As you walk around the shop, craftsmen are hard at work cutting, beating hammering, tinning, riveting and polishing pieces of copper. This is not just *pour le cinéma* (for show): l'Atelier du Cuivre has a big order book and some very serious customers.

It supplies Fouquet's in Paris and more locally, La Mère Poulard in Mont Saint Michel, home of the famously fluffy and much-imitated soufflé omelette. With its pans and utensils on sale throughout France, l'Atelier has twice appeared in the Guinness Book of Records, once for producing the largest-ever fish kettle and once for making the tiniest set of saucepans.

L'Atelier du Cuivre is the brainchild of two entrepreneurs and businessmen, Etienne Dullin and Yves Le Goupil. Some years ago they had the bright idea of opening up to the public an old workshop in order to make visitors understand and appreciate the old skills of the craft. In order that people could grasp the complicated process of copper working more easily, they also commissioned a seventeen-minute film. Videos of this nature tend to make me yawn with boredom and/or cringe with embarrassment, but I have to confess that I watched this one with pleasure twice in one day – once in French and once in English – in the interests of research. The video is very professionally made and explains the craft clearly and attractively, somehow managing to be evocative rather than corny. It is recommended viewing in either version.

A tour of the workshop certainly helps the visitor appreciate the value of hand-crafted copper utensils. It takes three-and-a-half hours to make a preserving pan. This is despite the fact that, unlike other pots and pans, rounded preserving pans do not need to be tinned (the sugar sticks to the tin and acts as a protective barrier). In all other cases, a layer of tin prevents the food from coming into contact with potentially toxic copper oxide.

In the context of the manufacture of culinary utensils, I was very interested by the tinning process as it closely resembles cooking. Tip a little tin into your pan, sauté it over a high heat for a few minutes, shaking the pan occasionally until it is evenly covered with molten tin. Then finish with a good rubbing of ammonia salt and wash thoroughly before use.

Amongst the shiny rows and piles of future sauté pans, fish kettles and preserving pans, a few battered-looking old pots looked less desirable. I was told that these had come in for repair. In January and February, old pans are brought or sent in for re-tinning and a spot of general maintenance. Re-tinning is a difficult job because the old copper surface is scratched and

The tinning process. Molten tin is swirled around the inside of the copper pan and allowed to cool. After being rubbed with ammonia salt, the pan is washed down before it joins a gleaming piles of articles ready for one more inspection.

A proud glistening tower of copper pans.

Assembling a small decorative wash basin.

Sauté pans waiting to be tinned.

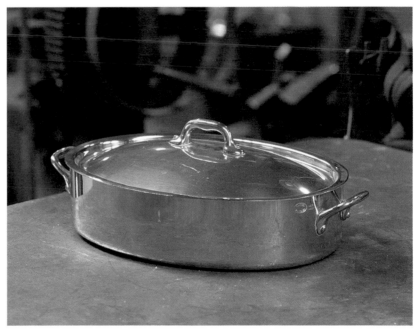

Waiting for the perfect turbot: an oval copper fish kettle in all its pristine glory.

damaged and the tin does not then stick well. It was, however, comforting to hear that it is still possible to get some things repaired.

In the glittering shop and showroom attached to the workshop I became the proud owner of a small, heavy saucepan – tin-lined, of course, but also nicely balanced and altogether professional. Was it going to need a lot of polishing? I asked, never having owned such a top-quality copper utensil before. Nothing to it, I was told. Use a commercial cleaner every now and then; unless you want to display your pan for decorative purposes, you don't need to polish it.

After a few months of regular use my little pan has become a favourite utensil. Because I am lazy, it hangs in the kitchen not exactly doing credit to my polishing skills. However, I reach for it every time I want to make a 'proper' little sauce. It handles well and it controls heat efficiently. More obscurely, it inspires me with confidence and, yes, the success rate is greater with it than without.

Hammering a decorative motif on to a platter.

When he found his traditional skills no longer in demand, Monsieur Porre swopped horseshoes for wrought-iron work and diversified into a successful new career. Once the village farrier, he still works in his original forge with his old tools.

## MEN OF IRON AND HORSES

In France, as elsewhere, the village blacksmith played a vital part in the life of the community. Not only did he make and maintain the tools needed to work the land, essential domestic utensils were also entrusted to him for repairs – if not actually made by him. Last but not least, he shod the horses and even knew how to cure them when they were ill. The official local expert on metals and on all matters equine, the French village blacksmith was *l'homme du fer et des chevaux*, the man of iron and horses.

At the end of the twentieth century he has become something of an anachronism. When the local blacksmith in my village near the Loire retired in the early Seventies he was not replaced. As children we had all watched Monsieur Gentil (Mr Nice was sweet-natured and well deserved his surname) apply the hot shoes to the hooves of fewer and fewer horses, breathing in the unique smell of burnt horn. He had willingly helped us with broken bicycles, lost keys and many of the 'Things That Didn't Work'.

Monsieur Gentil's generation was the last of the old-style village blacksmiths. Even if they have not abandoned the old forges, traditionally very accessible at the entrance to villages, the younger men have acquired new skills.

Take the case of Monsieur Porre. Together with his two sons he runs the forge in Fayence, between Grasse and Draguignan. He has been in business there for over forty years. When he first started work he wanted to become a baker, but this was during the war and there wasn't much flour around. So he was instead apprenticed to a farrier in Draguignan. His boss had been a sergeant in Saumur, home of the famed Cadre Noir and unrivalled capital of the French riding world.

Duly trained, Monsieur Porre became an expert farrier and this stood him in good stead when he settled in Fayence. There were still 600 working horses in the village at the end of the war. Even the *gendarmes* went on horseback and the price of horseshoes – just like the price of bread – was fixed by the government.

There still is a fading horseshoe above the forge, but it is quite some time since Monsieur Porre last bent over a hoof. Most of his working life is now spent fashioning wrought iron. Little by little as he became more skilled, his gates, balustrades, hoods, balconies and conservatories became increasingly popular in the region. He also makes fine stark wrought-iron furniture for an expensive gallery in Paris. He enjoys his re-conversion: the money is better, of course, and his new clients are more appreciative than the old horses.

## PEWTER

More malleable but less heat-conductive than copper, silver-grey pewter was also traditionally crafted in Villedieu. Enormously in demand in the Middle Ages and during the Renaissance as tableware and for medicinal purposes in the form of instruments and containers, pewter's popularity peaked in the seventeenth century. It was then gradually replaced on the table by glazed pottery.

In the early Sixties, it briefly came back into fashion, the perfect manifestation of the newly discovered old-fashioned country look then in its early infancy. No French *résidence secondaire*, no country restaurant of the Jacques Tati/Mon Oncle era was complete without a set of pewter tankards above the mantelpiece, or a pewter jug on a well-varnished dark wood chest. Nothing ages faster than the very fashionable: most pewter jugs and tankards have discreetly returned to attics and cellars to await another coming.

Opposite l'Atelier du Cuivre and also the brainchild of Messrs. Dulin and Le Goupil, La Maison de l'Etain, The House of Pewter, boasts a fine collection of pewter moulds and several interesting examples of pewter craft. Open every day, the collection includes some ornate art deco gems and a few stark modern pieces which are well worth viewing.

## THE KNIFE CAPITAL OF FRANCE

Thiers in the Auvergne, not far from Clermont-Ferrand and Vichy, is the acknowledged capital of the French knife industry responsible for around 65 per cent of the country's production.

As industrial towns go it will come as more than merely a pleasant surprise to the visitor. Spiralling up the mountain side, the narrow streets of the town are lined with half-timbered houses. Seen from a distance they could be built on top of one another and their faded colours are reminiscent of Venice. In some derelict little alley or abandoned courtyard, if you listen carefully away from the noise of the traffic, you'll hear the unmistakable whoosh of the river. The river Durolle runs fast and soft-watered and is the reason why, several centuries ago, Thiers became a knife-making centre. Many of the 16,000 inhabitants still work in the industry and many more will tell you that their grandad used to be a knife-grinder.

Very few knives are made by hand these days and some twelve years ago the Thiers municipal council grew concerned about the ever-dwindling number of artisans skilled enough to make a knife from start to finish – from the bar of raw steel to the smoothly polished handle.

In the old days, knife-making took place all over the town, each district carrying out one specialized stage of the process. In the surrounding countryside and down by the river were the workshops and factories where the hard work took place amidst deafening noise: the heating and hammering, the quenching and hardening. After extreme heat came extreme cold.

The grinding wheels were powered by the icy water of the Durolle and the men worked facing the stream, lying on their bellies on wooden planks holding the blade in front of them. This was dangerous work as the wheels occasionally exploded without apparent reason. The constant cold and damp also made it extremely unhealthy, and old photographs show that dogs were trained to lie across their masters' backs to keep them tolerably warm.

Not surprisingly, the better-off master-craftsmen and merchants had their workshops and shops further up the hill in more salubrious quarters. They tended to live above the shop, and many of the town houses have kept the big, wide ground-floor windows purpose-built at the time.

Rather than revive a number of scattered sites – a formidably expensive task – the council prudently decided to concentrate its efforts on recreating two workshops which are now both open to the public. The first and more *folklorique* is in the heart of the old city, next to the Maison de l'Homme de Bois, the House of the Wooden Man (a legendary hairy-looking local character not unlike a distant cousin of the Green Man). It is an old-style grinding shop, where artisans grind and polish blades in the traditional way for the benefit of visitors.

The main site further up the street, aptly renamed Rue de la Coutellerie, is the Maison des Couteliers, the House of the Knife Makers. Here skilled artisans hand-make knives in front of visitors. Using modern and old techniques, they fashion traditional and experimental materials into knives. At the same time the Maison des Couteliers is both a busy commercial workshop – making knives to order – and a research laboratory. It also houses a shop and a very well-designed museum packed with fascinating exhibits, from medieval knife-makers' signs and hallmarks to the latest compounds that will be used to craft the knives of the future.

With its timbered buildings and winding narrow streets, the old town centre of Thiers is worth the steep climb.

## FRANCE'S ANSWER TO THE SWISS ARMY KNIFE

In the windows of Thiers' innumerable knife shops, on display at the Maison de la Coutellerie, on sale at knife stalls all over France on market days, you cannot fail to see the *laguiole*, a distinctive clasp knife which is slim-profiled, slightly curved, with a horn or ivory handle and three visible rivets.

France's answer to the Swiss Army Knife is named after the village in which it was first manufactured early in the last century, Laguiole in the Aveyron north of Rodez. This is rugged cattle and sheep country and the knife was carried by shepherds.

In addition to the main blade, the *laguiole* traditionally had a separate pointed spike, useful for piercing a hole into the gut of greedy animals in danger of bursting after eating too much lucerne. It was also used for removing small stones from horses' shoes. In our more pleasure-oriented society, this spike is often replaced by a corkscrew.

Easy-to-handle and highly efficient, the *laguiole* is a very popular all-purpose *couteau de poche* (pocket knife). The word *laguiole* (note the small 'l') is not a trademark but simply a description of the shape of the knife. My guide at Thiers told me that over 90 per cent of *laguioles* were in fact manufactured in Thiers.

However, we are in the country of the Appellation Contrôlée. The Aveyron council recently decided to re-launch the *laguiole* where it truly belongs – in Laguiole. A group of local artisans (trained in Thiers) have opened their own workshop and a new factory produces a born-again *laguiole*, re-designed by Philippe Starck.

Inspired by the success of the traditional knife-making revival at the Maison des Couteliers, is Laguiole about to embark on a craft war against Thiers? France is a big enough country to take both and the two places are far enough apart. Let us also not forget that when they start a fight the French draw metaphorical knives rather than daggers.

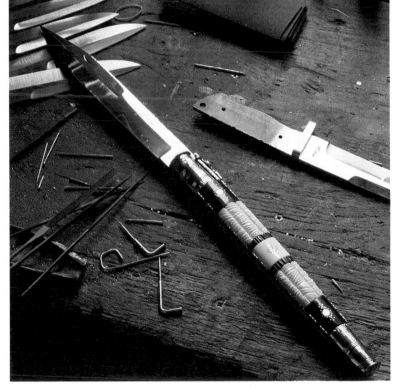

*Opposite and above* Inside the Maison des Couteliers, ears well muffled against the noise and totally oblivious of visitors, a craftsman hones a series of knives.

*Right* Two collector's pieces: made-to-order hunting knife (*top*) and a genuine masterpiece. This ornate knife in the Spanish style took an aspiring master craftsman two weeks to make.

I particularly enjoyed looking at the displays of the miniatures the knife-makers used to craft in their very limited hours of leisure. Leftover scraps of metal, horn, bone and ivory were hoarded (with the consent of the management – this was a small perk that went with the job) and painstakingly crafted into tiny snuff-boxes, purses or exquisite bottles which would not have been out of place in an smart goldsmith's window.

Modestly displayed in a shop window, an assortment of *laguioles* and pocket knives.

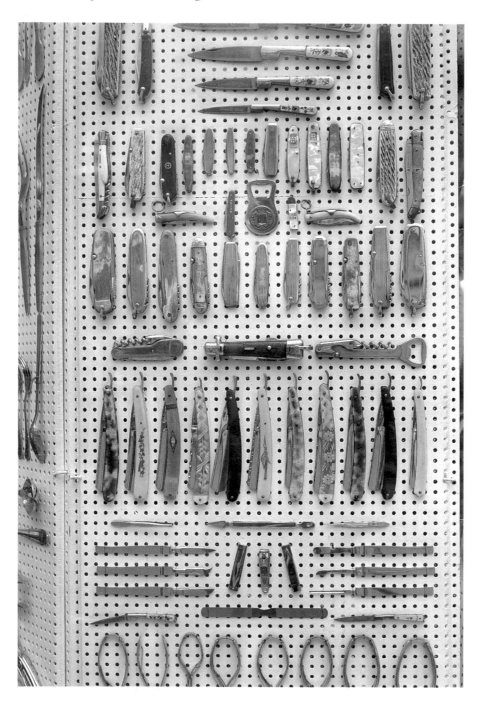

## THE BELL FOUNDRY

Perhaps because of a long and deeply rooted Catholic tradition, France – the oldest daughter of the Church of Rome – has always been a country renowned for the quality of its bell-making. To this day several foundries are still busily casting in time-honoured tradition. Bells are being made in Saint-Jean de Braye in Burgundy and in the Jura at the Paccard foundry in Annecy – birthplace, incidentally, of Philadelphia's famous Liberty Bell.

Another high spot in the register of French bell foundries is Villedieu-les-Poêles which will not come as a surprise if you consider the city's long tradition of metal-working. The Cornille-Havard works in the rue du Pont-Chignon, not far from the river, were built in 1862. If this seems somewhat late in the history of old Villedieu, this is because bell-founders used to be itinerant artisans, travelling the roads of Europe, setting up their tools and digging their pits as close as possible to the church or cathedral for which their bells were destined. Sensible enough when you remember that 500 kilos (half a ton) is not really a heavy weight for a largish bell.

The advent of the railways changed everything. Bell-casters began to stay in the same place and work in 'factories'. Even in the age of railways, however, transporting bells has remained an arduous business. When a bell weighing several tons had to find its way from the Paccard foundry to the Sacré-Coeur Basilica in Montmartre at the end of the last century, the railway did not go quite far enough. Some forty oxen had to pull the huge bell up the steep hill. There still is no railway station at the top of Montmartre and I wonder if a modern juggernaut could manage both the weight of the bell and the narrow streets? Fortunately bells live to a ripe old age before they need any further attention.

The Cornille-Havard foundry is open to the public and is a fascinating place to visit. If you want to purchase a bell, there is a well-stocked shop with all manners of bells and attractive bronze and copper objects on display. Whether or not the assistant manages to persuade you that every home needs its own bell, you must take time to go round the foundry. It is well set back from the street, on what feels like the edge of the old city. You walk through a fine town-house archway that could be straight out of *Madame Bovary*, into a short gravel drive and forecourt featuring the odd cracked bell and some abandoned tools. Here you are in for a bit of a visual surprise: as the factory building looms large and severe, with its touches of green paint around the windows, its imposing clock, very high chimney and generally rugged character, it is strikingly attractive but totally unexpected. I was reminded of old-fashioned factories in the Vosges. Somehow this stern powerful appearance was unlike anything else I had seen in amiable Normandy.

But then the whole process of bell making is a truly paradoxical one,

The tall square tower of the Eglise Notre-Dame gracefully dominates Villedieu-les-Poêles.

Inside the Cornille-Havard foundry: an abandoned mould and a brand new bell.

involving as it does huge quantities of molten metal which somehow coalesce into a musical instrument that hits just the right note. Inferno and fine tuning... a bell's tonality is fixed once and for all when the bronze is poured into the mould. Stranger still, at Cornille-Havard the making of any given bell involves tools of the trade as diverse as goat's hair and horse manure and a microcomputer and an electronic spectrum analyser.

Given a few local variations, people in the north tend to like their bells thicker than southerners do. On the whole the shape of bells and the way they are made have changed very little in the last five hundred years. The problem with bell-making is the eternal one of building a mould with enough precision, so that when the metal is poured into it the resulting bell has just the right tonality.

Once the bell is cast, there are no second chances: a bell that does not produce the right sound, or one that breaks or cracks when it emerges from the mould can never be melted down again to make another bell. (The bronze used at Cornille-Havard for casting is a special alloy of 78 per cent copper with 22 per cent tin.) I had visions of solid lakes of wasted metal, but my guide reassured me that leftover or recovered bronze can be made into other utensils and is also used for decorative purposes.

Perfection for perfection's sake (*left*).
Once a bell is installed in a belfry,
its exquisite decorations and
inscriptions will not be seen again.

Still in the casting pit (*left*), a bell,
newly cast and waiting to be
polished to a gleaming finish (*right*).
Not all bells survive the drama of
casting: the unlucky ones are
melted down again and their alloy
is used for other purposes.

Finely tuned, inscribed to the client's wishes and polished to a glossy finish, these two bells are ready for dispatch.

With great fervour, the foundry guide shepherds her visitors among working artisans, explaining the complicated process in very clear and simple terms. If something is not happening on the day you visit the works, there are plenty of models and replicas to help you get a good idea of what goes on.

The whole bell-making procedure starts with a central mould to form the interior shape of the bell. Following an ancient formula, this core is gradually built up with a mixture of clay, horse or pigs' hair and manure smoothed on to kind of precisely measured heavy-duty template, gives the bell its inner profile. The clay and manure loam is dried by lighting a light charcoal fire inside the core and the whole surface is then coated with soot and given a smooth finish. The outside gauge – the exterior profile of the bell – is cut and fixed to the axle.

At this stage something called the 'false bell' is built, again with several layers of clay mixture. This false bell is covered with tallow on which are laid decorations and inscriptions stamped in wax. Last comes the cope, a thick outer crust of manure and clay, and to cap the main structure, the mould for the crown of the bell is built on top. Heating makes the wax and tallow melt and the cope may then be opened and the loosened false bell is broken and discarded. In the space left by the false bell will be poured the bronze that turns into the real bell.

Now comes the truly spectacular part – the drama of casting. The bronze alloy is heated, in a huge furnace for large bells and in a melting-pot for more modest ones, until it reaches 1100°C (2000°F). It is normal practice to cast several bells at the same time. After the prolonged slow process of moulding, casting has to take place in one go – in a matter of a minute or so. So that the moulds can take the enormous impact and pressure of the torrent of molten metal without exploding (at the bottom of the mould the pressure is thirteen times the weight of the bell) they are buried deep in pits of packed earth.

The liquid bronze pours in from the furnace through brick channels, the funnels into the bell mould are opened and fireworks literally take place as the air in the mould is pushed out and replaced by incandescent metal. I was quite willing to believe my mentor when she told me that during casting

Whereas church bells tend to be inscribed in Latin, lay clients often want their bells to be decorated with coats of arms.

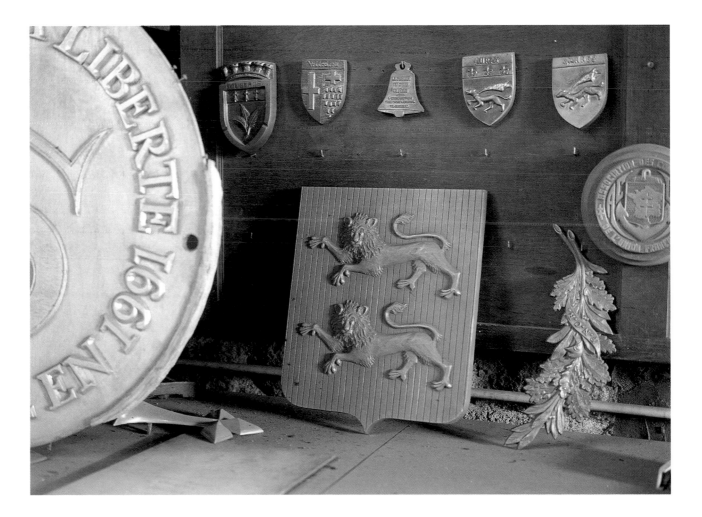

flames will soar 4–5 metres (13–16 feet) above the 20-metre (66-feet) tall chimney I had earlier found so impressive.

And calm of mind, all passion spent… what follows has to be something of an anticlimax. The day after the casting the earth around the moulds is removed and the moulds are left to cool, sometimes for as long as two weeks if the bells are large.

Then comes another nail-biting episode; the cope is broken with axes and the bell revealed in all its burnt and blackened glory. It will then be painstakingly sanded, smoothed and polished. It will also be checked for sound – this is where the electronic spectrum analyser comes in – and fine-tuned, sometimes with a little internal filing. Once the various accessories have been fitted and the steel clapper has been attached, the brand new bell will be dispatched to its destination, to ring and peal truthfully for a couple of centuries.

The next time I plan a visit to Villedieu I shall do my utmost to make it happen on a day Cornille-Havard are casting a batch of bells.

## A MUSICAL INSTRUMENT

The note sounded by a bell will depend on its diameter at the base and on the ratio of thickness to diameter where the clapper strikes the bell. The larger the diameter the deeper the note, and the thicker the bell the higher the note.

In the Christian tradition a bell is tuned to one of five notes: 'nominal', 'fundamental', 'hum', 'minor third' and 'fifth'. It may be rung on its own or with other bells, with different sizes and tonalities. In a chime, the various bells are struck in succession and play the same melody, while in a more complex carillon the bells are played at the same time, in concordance, controlled by a keyboard.

## THE STONES OF THE AUVERGNE

The rare precious and semi-precious stones that were used by artisans to make traditional jewellery varied a great deal from region to region. What was crafted depended very much on what the area had to offer, that is, what ore and materials could be extracted locally. There was rock crystal in the Alps, garnet and pink quartz in several places and rhodonite in the Pyrenees. Mother-of-pearl from certain types of shellfish was also used in Corsica.

An abundance of riches: cut and uncut stones from the depths of the Auvergne.

Many of the minerals from the Auvergne so confidently lined up in this display case at the end of the last century are no longer to be found.

Probably the richest region of all when it came to minerals was the land of the ancient volcanoes, the Auvergne. Two centuries ago it was not unusual for someone to hit on a rich seam by accident. Purple-hued amethyst was a particularly common find – so much so that it became known as the Stone of the Auvergne and was not greatly prized. The stones used to be sent to not-too-distant Switzerland to be cut and set.

About a century ago, the Taillerie de Royat, just outside Clermont-Ferrand, became one of the first workshops to cut and fashion local stones. The seams of precious and semi-precious stones are long since exhausted, but the Taillerie still provides a unique introduction to the ancient skills of stone-cutting. The shop and workshop are both housed in an ornate tall building of brick and varied stones set on the side of a steep road. A fast-streaming river called the Tiretaine runs on the other side. It was well into spring when we visited, but the cars coming down from the hilltops were all laden with snow and the air was chilly on the river bank.

The shop is a large room with two tall cashier's desks, a high ceiling, painted local scenes above the doors, old school wall charts showing the various stones and last – but best of all – dozens of splendid wood cabinets and glass cases packed with glittering stones and jewellery. They are arranged by colour and type of stone: here you see the agate family: black onyx, lovely blue chalcedony, red cornelian; there is amethyst; over there is jasper in red, blue and yellow; back over here is rosy tourmaline, delicately green aventurine and brilliant rock crystal … it was like stepping into the set for a turn-of-the-century costume drama.

The shop and workshop are run as a family business by Madame Noir and her daughter, assisted by two local craftswomen who have worked at the Taillerie since they were fourteen. One of them also acts as a guide for the visitors who go backstage into the workshop.

Rather like the knives at Thiers, the stones were traditionally cut by artisans half-lying, half-kneeling for maximum arm-power. Supported by wooden benches, they faced the sandstone wheels which were powered by the Tiretaine. As the stones get more and more finished, they progress from being worked on against a large wheel with a coarse surface to smaller wheels with a fine grain. By the polishing stage, ground ruby is used as the polishing agent, always with a trickle of water to keep the temperature down.

After the cutting shop some of the stones, now with many glittering facets, are mounted into rings and brooches or strung into necklaces and bracelets. Bigger pieces are made into ashtrays, paperweights or book ends. Many cut stones are left loose, *au naturel,* for customers to set or use as they wish. Some stones are now used for medicinal purposes: people increasingly buy rock crystals or amethysts for their reputed healing or health-giving properties.

I was astonished by the wonderful ornaments and pieces of jewellery crammed into a rather dusty storeroom next to the workshop. Why were they

*Above left* Old fashioned polishing wheels in the Royat Taillerie.

*Below left* Assorted rough-hewn stone ashtrays and candlesticks.

*Above right* A fine large piece of amethyst, a popular stone once commonly found in the Auvergne, takes pride of place in this casual window-sill display.

*Below right* Cut stones are mounted into rings at apron-shaped work benches.

Delicate jewellery is temptingly displayed in handsome old-fashioned cases.

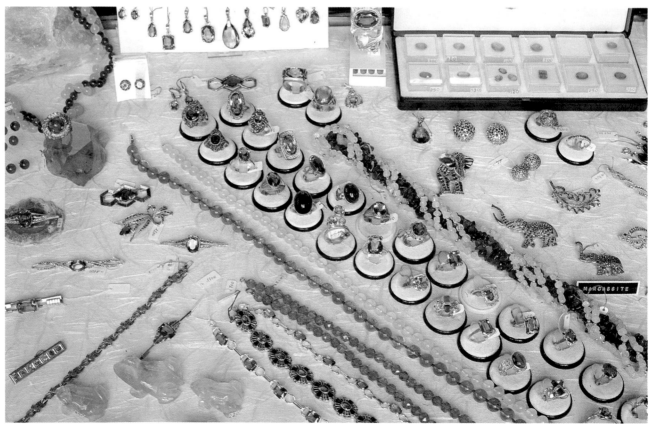

not displayed in the shop? Madame Noir's daughter explained with a smile that what was in the shop was only the tip of the iceberg. The Taillerie's stock of stones is very large. Madame Noir, now in her eighties, hates the idea of parting with the stones and jewels of which she is particularly proud. 'If they are very beautiful, somehow my mother prefers to keep them here. It would break her heart if she had to let go of some pieces.' A walk-in jewellery box…

Religious medals from Bernard Lissague's unique collection.

## MEDALS AND RELIGIOUS ART

Rosary beads, crucifixes, medals, statuettes and all such religious articles have been made in France for centuries. Grand pieces were fashioned in the precious materials used by jewellers and goldsmiths, like ivory, platinum, gold, silver, mother-of-pearl and cultivated pearls. More frequently, the making of rosary beads was a real cottage industry. Around such towns as Ambert in the Auvergne and Saumur on the Loire at the meeting point of Anjou and Touraine, it kept hundreds of out-workers busy stringing and polishing little balls of boxwood, bone and coconut.

A few kilometres north of Saumur, just west of the prosperous vineyards of Bourgueil and Saint-Nicolas de Bourgueil – perhaps after a spot of *dégustation* – visitors interested in the story of religious articles will find the village of Brain-sur-Allonnes. It is the home of the Nouvelle Société Mayaud, where a staff of thirty-six are still using traditional methods and original old moulds to turn out medals and statuettes. The pious and the profane mix happily in the

*Left* Statuettes of the Virgin and Child fresh from the casting mould.

Société's showroom: sporting trophies, cups and corporate gifts nowadays play a significant part in the turnover.

Owner Bernard Lissague is justly proud of his enormous collection of hundreds of moulds and thousands of medals. Not far from the workshops, he also has a unique private museum of religious art. It houses some 200,000 exhibits – many of them in boxes because of the shortage of space. Some of the items on display are beautiful examples of the religious artisans' skills: delicate crucifixes resting on faded velvet or rosary beads made of exquisite pearls. Some look mysterious: like the drum (not unlike a cement-mixer or something out of which an innocent hand will draw a winning number) that was used for polishing beads with ground pumice stone, an ancient foot-lathe... Others are more bizarre still: like the order book of one of the old Société Maillaud's salesmen a century and a half ago. A veritable missionary, he travelled with coffers full of samples to the American mid-West, South America and Central Africa, reporting his progress in a laboured long-hand.

Assorted medals and votaries from the Lissague collection.

# GLASS

Where does craft end and art begin? This question has exercised the minds of many over the years and generated furiously heated debate. To make matters worse, in French the word for craft – *l'artisanat* – is obviously derived from the word *l'art*… If you ever stop to wonder whether the *artisan*, the craftsman, is some humble relative of the artist, *l'artiste*, you can then get into an animated discussion about *métiers d'art* – where high craft becomes decorative art! The dictionary helpfully translates the all-purpose word *métier* as trade, job, profession, occupation and craft.

Perhaps more in the area of glass than in any of the other crafts discussed in this book, does the *art/artisanat* problem become an issue. People involved in the *métier* expressed very different opinions. When it came to stained glass, only the painter creating the original design was considered an artist. In Biot it seemed that the glass-blowers were encouraged to experiment along artistic lines in their spare time if they so wished. Baccarat employs designers alongside artisans and its policy is to encourage craftsmen to develop their skills and expertise to the full, and at Dieulefit a genuine artisan workshop has imperceptibly moved into producing art glass.

*Vive la différence*! Whether art or craft, traditional or experimental, there is much French glass of all types to enjoy throughout the country.

## THE SPIRITUAL CAPITAL OF
## FRENCH STAINED GLASS

Gloriously playing with the sunlight, the great windows of Chartres Cathedral are some of the finest examples of the art of the stained glass craftsmen.

In the rich plain of the Beauce – in whichever direction you are travelling, south from Paris, east from Normandy or north from Orléans and the central Loire – Chartres Cathedral from the distance will first seem like a child's drawing of a church, a pointed triangle on top of one end of a rectangle, obviously getting bigger as you approach. However, by the time you slow down in the traffic of the city suburbs, it will have totally disappeared. Only when you look up in the centre of the town will you suddenly see the Cathedral again, looming high up and very large. From now on it will catch your eye when you least expect it, discreetly dominating its city from a rocky pedestal.

To experience the Cathedral in all its glory, it is best to go in late on a sunny afternoon, when the light pours in through the stained glass windows and plays like wildfire on arches and paving stones. The stained glass windows at Chartres, many freshly restored to their earlier brilliance, are amongst the most magnificent in the country. The city is the spiritual capital of French stained glass – no mean feat when you bear in mind that France has more stained glass than the rest of the world put together.

Chartres seemed a good place to start exploring the country's traditional glass crafts. In medieval times, the most beautiful works of glass in western

The tranquil gardens of the Atelier Lorin, with a glimpse of the Cathedral steeples in the distance.

At close range, the dramatic buttresses of the Cathedral tower above the quieter façades of the surrounding buildings.

A tall transept window casting a mysterious glow into the Cathedral.

All the light the day has to offer pours into the main workshop, enabling craftsmen to work with stained glass in the right environment.

Europe were the windows created to bring light into the great cathedrals. Blown glass could never be made into sheets large enough to cover the span between the arches, so smaller pieces were held together by lead, that most flexible of metals.

The need to have small pieces of glass held together by a dark armature was – in true artisan fashion – turned into an advantage by the use of glass of different colours. Patterns added variety and richness, designs created pictures that came to life with the light from outside.

As a result of the importance of stained glass, coloured glass was constantly experimented with and perfected by master-glaziers. There still are a hundred or so of them in France and the profession now has a meeting place in Chartres which is also open to the public. At the Centre International du Vitrail, in an eighteenth-century crypt and granary close by the Cathedral, visitors can find out about the ancient craft of stained glass and the work of modern master-glaziers. Audio-visual shows, exhibitions, a library and multi-lingual book shop provide up-to-date and thorough information.

If you want to see traditional stained glass in the making, walk down to the rue de la Tannerie, a pretty street of old buildings, narrow bridges and abandoned wash-houses along a branch of the river Eure. There at number 46 is the Atelier Lorin, stained glass makers for well over a century. The glassworks replaced an old tannery and some of the buildings go back to the sixteenth century.

Everything still looks as if it had been there for centuries: the storeroom with its dusty sheets and broken pieces of multi-coloured glass in ancient wooden cases, the creaky external staircase and rickety gallery that take you to the workshop where the glass is cut and the lead fitted. A radio quietly playing somewhere in the background strikes the only noticeably modern note. There is a touch of Sleeping Beauty's Castle about the place, but then stained glass is not made overnight. Large orders take several years – sometimes over a decade – to complete. Master-glaziers have always tended to work *pour l'avenir*, for future generations…

The first stage in the process of stained-glass making consists of a colour sketch, drawn on paper to one-tenth of the scale of the proposed piece. From this is drawn a life-size cartoon using charcoal or China ink, which is then copied on to tracing paper and finally transferred on to strong card to make a template. This template is cut to look just like a jigsaw puzzle with numbered

Luminous piece after luminous piece, the intricate stained glass jigsaw is assembled.

Once loosely assembled, the stained glass panels are tested for colour in a tall-ceilinged narrow room known as *la tour*, the tower.

*Left* In the workshop pieces of coloured glass are cut to match the numbered templates.

*Right* Every colour in the rainbow: samples of stained glass mouth-blown in the traditional way. The tiny irregularities allow the light to play more naturally.

pieces. These numbered pieces are assembled on the tracing paper, each ready to be used as a pattern for a single piece of glass in the window.

Whenever possible, artisans use sunlight to select glass and to check colours, constantly holding pieces up against the light. The main workshop at the Atelier Lorin has huge windows running along its entire length, letting in plenty of morning light. Before the lead is finally fixed into place, larger stained glass works are assembled, panel by panel, against a wall of plain glass (again facing the best available light) in a tall narrow room known as *la Tour*, the Tower. Equipped with a wooden platform on a winch and a primitive-looking man-of-war to enable the artisans to reach the top of the tall windows, the tower has a timeless feel. There colours are painstakingly checked against the sky and against the original sketch, often for hours on end as the light changes.

Does the Atelier Lorin work for individual customers? Yes, they are happy to take 'private' orders, but prices tend to be high. Coloured blown glass is very expensive and the process of assembling pieces of glass and ribbons of lead into a complex and luminous picture is lengthy. Alas and alack…

In one of the rooms, a striking secular piece by the Atelier Lorin from the late nineteenth century.

A cylinder of antique coloured glass mouth-blown in the traditional way. The cylinders are cut open and flattened into sheets.

Left over or broken fragments of expensive stained glass seldom get thrown away. However small, there is always a chance that they might fit into a design.

## SHEETS OF ANTIQUE GLASS

Only one single glassworks in France produces the sheets of 'antique' coloured glass that are used for making traditional stained glass windows or motifs. The Verrerie de Saint-Just is in the Haute-Loire near Saint Etienne. Here coloured glass for cathedral windows has been mouth-blown ever since the seventeenth century.

More or less the same techniques are still used at Saint-Just. From the pots of incandescent liquefied mass, the glass blower gradually collects a smooth heavy ball weighing around 7 kilos (15 lb) on the end of a long hollow rod. This fiery globe he blows into a fat cylinder, known as a *manchon* or muff. The cylinder is cut off at both ends and split down the middle. After being re-heated until it once more becomes soft enough to work with, it is opened and flattened into a sheet of glass.

More often than not the glass is coloured throughout by metallic oxides. Tiny bubbles and scratches are built in: these intentional 'imperfections' give the glass its antique appearance and texture. More important still, they help capture and reflect the light, giving depth and interest where 'perfect' glass might just look flat.

After such a labour-intensive process it is no wonder that the sheets of glass, which are around 4 mm ($\frac{1}{6}$ in) thick and measure 60 x 80 cm (24 x 32 in), cost a great deal of money. They are hoarded like gold dust by the stained glass workshops and practically no fragment gets thrown away – even the tiniest piece is kept for future use.

## THE GLASS OF BIOT

From the religious to the secular, from the serious centre of the country to its smiling south, my voyage around French glass-making next took me to Biot, a few kilometres outside Antibes.

If you say the word Biot to a French person with a question mark in your voice, the chances are that he or she will reply *verre* or *verrerie* – glass or glassworks. Once synonymous with the tall jars in which olive oil used to be stored (see page 43*ff*), Biot has become the home of French *verre artisanal*, hand-crafted glass.

Let me begin with a little potted history. The Provençal glass-making tradition goes back several centuries. Gentlemen glass-makers (glass-making was the prerogative of the aristocracy until the Revolution) set up kilns in the pine forests, moving on to new sites when they ran out of the wood needed to keep the kiln at 1400°C (2550°F) long enough to turn the magic mixture of sand, lime and soda into a fiery mass of molten glass. The development of industrial glass put an end to their activities, and the last of the old-style Provençal glassworks in La Bocca just outside Cannes closed in 1899. Bottles, glasses, jars, demijohns, flagons and oil-lamps had all become mass-produced.

In 1956 there came to Biot a ceramicist with a vision, Eloi Monod, who decided to set up shop in the town to make the traditional glass utensils of Provence in a traditional way. He wanted his glass to be 'real country glass, blown and hand-crafted'. From his travels around craft glassworks in Spain and Italy, Monod had brought back a love of the old blown glass with its bubbles and imperfections. He had the idea of imitating the old-fashioned bubbled look and what was an accident he turned into a technique.

The first 'layer' of molten glass still on the tip of the blowpipe is dusted with a little carbonate of soda. More incandescent glass paste is then scooped up from the kiln and swirled over the carbonate. Through contact with the heat, the trapped carbonate of soda produces tiny bubbles of carbon dioxide. When glass is faulty, the carbon dioxide bubbles often break up to the surface, making the glass rough to the touch and likely to chip. The glass of Biot, however, has a smooth finish and the bubbles – like the colour – are safely ensconced within its substance.

The small bubbles, all playing up a little differently, were an instant success. The bubbled glass of Biot was born and the look has been much imitated. As Monod was the first to admit, however, it's only too easy to overdo it… a few bubbles go a long way. Monod's successors at the Verrerie, Danièle Lechaczynski and her husband Jean, have continued producing glass very much in the same way. First and foremost the workshop is open to the public, just as it was in the days of Monod.

Of all the live shows the various crafts can offer visitors, glass-making is

The stately ballet of the glass-blowers begins the moment the ball of glass is collected from the kiln …

Glass cools and hardens quickly. During the blowing process it has to be reheated every now and then to bring it back to working temperature – between 800° and 1100°C (1472°–2012°F).

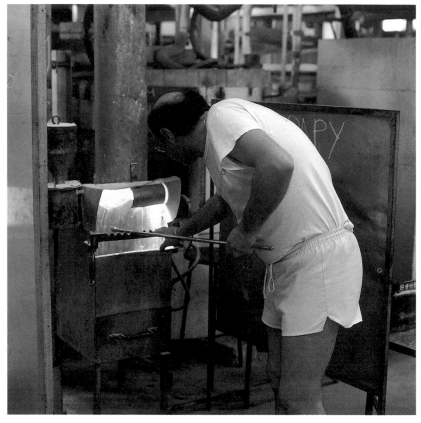

without question the most spectacular. Like so many pied pipers, the artisans come and go in balletic fashion, intensely absorbed by their long steel rods carrying incandescent bulbs.

There is a trick when watching a new game – concentrate on what one particular player is doing rather than try to take in the whole of the action. After watching the mesmerizing dance for a few minutes, I heeded Danièle Lechaczynski's advice and concentrated on a small red ball of molten glass from the moment it was picked up from the mouth of the kiln on the tip of a blowpipe, turning round and round lest it should drip like honey. This then gets transferred to a cast-iron surface, still turning round and round. Looking smoother, it suddenly becomes bigger and turns into an orange-red candle bulb. I looked back and up. The blowing had started.

There follows the sprinkling with carbonate of soda, and then the glass changes hands. Each piece of glass is made by a team of three artisans. The first one, the least experienced, is known as *le gamin*, the lad. Next comes the mate or assistant, *l'aide*, now sitting and rolling the rod along bars while shaping the glass with a scoop-like mould, then with pincers, all the while occasionally blowing air into it. The neck is indented where it will be cut, but

The *maître verrier*, the master glass-blower, carries out the more difficult jobs. He gently blows into the rod, keeps it rotating and coaxes the glass into shape with pincers.

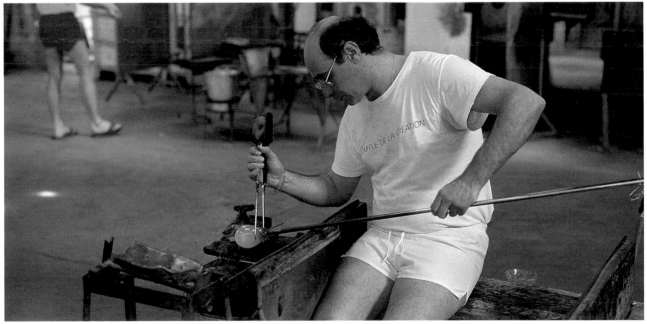

To give the glass a smooth even shape it is essential that the blowpipe be kept continuously rotating, even as the rim is cut and trimmed with scissors. The ribbon of excess glass which flops off has the texture of soft caramel.

the hardening cooling glass has already turned yellow. The assistant dips it into a separate small re-heating kiln. At this point the most senior member of the team, the master glass-maker, *le maître verrier* takes over and with swift flowing gestures and precise movements of pincers, irons, palette and mould, gives the piece of glass its final shape, occasionally putting it briefly into the re-heating kiln.

It all looked so simple and easy that it came as no surprise to be told that it takes nearly ten years to become a master glass-maker. At Biot there are twenty such skilled artisans – of different ages to ensure continuity. In fact, the last member of Monod's team from the Fifties retired only last year.

Finished glass slowly cools in the *arche*, a tunnel-shaped oven with a conveyor belt, starting at a temperature of 500°C (930°F) and finishing eight or ten hours later at 25°C (77°F). Finally comes the engraved sand-blasted signature, without which no piece leaves the Biot works.

Very few of the million or so people who visit Biot every year (the great majority come in July and August and during the French Christmas and Easter school holidays) leave without purchasing something. After watching the glass being made, visitors find themselves in the spacious and airy shop, which has a cool atrium in the centre. There temptation awaits in many shapes and sizes and in nine delicious colours: rosa quartz, amethyst and amber, clear glass, blue and Persian blue, lime, green and chartreuse. Pitchers, jugs, bowls, cups, tumblers, ladles, preserving pots, jars, stemmed glasses, candle-lamps… the whole range of the articles made at Biot is available in all nine colours.

Any best sellers? I was told that there were some seasonal variations. Delicate green, lime, rosa quartz and clear glass are always popular, but the strong Persian blue goes well in summer. It is a deep luminous colour that seems to be leaping out of a painting by Matisse. Apparently Jackie Onassis was so taken with it that she commissioned several days' worth of *Bleu de Perse* production.

The Lechaczynskis' approach to marketing is as skilled and down-to-earth as the glass-making craft of the artisans who work at Biot. For Monsieur Lechaczynski, marketing is a *sine qua non* of craftsmanship: 'There is no such thing as a confidential artisan. If nobody knows about the product, if there is no one able to sell the glass made by our artisans, then we'll all have to close up shop. If the marketing network isn't there, the craft will simply disappear.' He feels that far too many skills and traditions have vanished as a result of either poor marketing or of some insidious form of elitism – a snobby desire to keep the craft a well-kept secret.

Lechaczynski makes no bones of the fact that he comes from a management culture and would have found it just as easy to sell, say, sausages as he did glass, enjoying the problem solving and the human element. Just like his wife, however, he gradually became passionate about the material, working

assiduously to turn Biot into an internationally recognized centre of glass excellence. First there was the serious problem of training and keeping the best artisans. Much was done to make working conditions as attractive as possible, but some initiatives were strongly resisted.

Take, for example, the business of the curtain of water. On a visit to Monsieur Morin in Dieulefit (see page 109), the Lechaczynskis had been very impressed by a gadget he had devised. This consisted of installing a cooling curtain of water in front of the kilns to palliate the extreme heat of the glasshouse. The proposed improvement was not greeted with enthusiasm. Nonsense, said the Biot artisans. We are glass-makers, we can take the heat…!

The Lechaczynskis also encouraged the glass-blowers' creativity by promoting the old tradition of *bousillage*, the possibility for each artisan to use kiln and glass in his own time for his own ends. A number of such experiments have found a place in the exhibition galleries at the Verrerie.

The dividing line between craft and art is a thin, elastic one. A former apprentice, Jean-Claude Novaro, who started work in the glasshouse when he was 14, went on to become one of the leading glass artists in France. He now has his own studio, also in Biot, and the first exhibition gallery to be built

Glass-blowing is fascinating to watch. After such a great show, even the most budget-conscious of visitors will be tempted to open his or her purse. The shop is packed with colourful rows of attractive bubble glassware. If you look very carefully, you'll find that no two pieces are entirely identical – the tiny captive air bubbles pop up just a little differently in each glass.

For many of its loyal fans, Biot
means very well-made rustic glass
with bubbles and strong rounded
shapes, like these classic water jugs
(*right*). The Lechaczynskis have
recently introduced new lines, such
as delicate clouded glass and fine
chinaware decorated with traditional
Provençal patterns (*opposite*).

at the Verrerie was named after him. To the Galerie Jean-Claude Novaro has recently been added a museum of contemporary glass, La Galerie Internationale du Verre, where works by modern masters are exhibited.

The Lechaczynskis now have a son and daughter working with them in the family business, and it seems that Biot is very much there to stay on the world map of glass. As I was getting ready to leave, Monsieur Lechaczynski told me about another local craft that had not fared so well, that of the *pierres à four*, stones for the bakers' oven. The last of the artisans had apparently closed up his business... Was the Verrerie contemplating a little diversification, I wondered as I left.

## MEILLEURS OUVRIERS DE FRANCE

There are several thousand people in France with the title of *Un des Meilleurs Ouvriers de France* (One of the Best Workmen in France) and, if you look carefully on shop windows and letter heads, sooner or later you are bound to come across a laureate.

He or she may be a plumber or a hairdresser, a pâtissier or a photographer, a glass engraver or a cabinet-maker, a lace-maker or a florist, a taxidermist or a knife-maker. Whatever the line of work, one thing is guaranteed: he or she will be very good at his or her job. It takes a long time and a lot of hard work to become *Un des Meilleurs Ouvriers*. Candidates competing for the title – and the medal with a coloured ribbon that goes with it – in any of over 200 different disciplines have to show a great deal of patient determination. Many of the initially unsuccessful ones give the exam another try.

The competition is a relatively recent one, started in the Twenties, originally with an exhibition of masterpieces, to promote the cause of manual workers and the love of work well done. It encourages the upkeep and continuation of traditional expertise and the development of modern skills. Halfway between an exam and a competition and sponsored by several official bodies (including the Ministry of Education), it is a lengthy procedure, with strict and involved regulations, that takes place in different stages over a three-year period.

Candidates have to carry out a set task, one that challenges their complete mastery of the subject. In a second and more purely competitive phase, they are judged on their creative skills as exhibited in a project of their choice. The juries include representatives of the profession as well as other Meilleurs Ouvriers, past winners in the same category.

The title carries great kudos and greatly enhances the career prospects of the winners. The network of the multi-disciplinary Meilleurs Ouvriers is strong and tightly-knit, the 'old boys' enjoying working with and for their peers and fellow top craftsmen.

## THE CRYSTAL OF BACCARAT

Famed for the beauty of its stained glass and mirror glass, France was a relatively late developer when it came to fine vessel glass. This was because the monarchs and their courts, always fashion leaders, tended to favour the glass of Bohemia, which was brilliantly clear and richly cut in colours that emulated precious stones.

In 1764 the Bishop of Metz asked for Louis XV's authority to open a glassworks in Baccarat, in Lorraine. The owner of the estate and vast forests in the Vosges, the astute Bishop used a convincing argument, pointing out that the import of glass from Bohemia was depleting the royal coffers, 'at a time when the kingdom has a great need of funds to recover from the terrible Seven Year's War'. What could the King do but grant the Bishop's request. The Baccarat glassworks opened and prospered, producing goblets, mirrors and window glass until the Revolution.

In 1817 production switched to lead crystal. The formula for lead crystal had been developed by the English glass-maker George Ravenscroft in 1676. It was known in France, and the Saint-Louis glassworks, also in Lorraine, had been making crystal since 1781. During the nineteenth century, the names of Saint-Louis and Baccarat, busily competing against the then preeminent Bohemia and England, became known throughout the elegant world. Lorraine swiftly became the home of French crystal, which it has remained to this day. Competitive from the very beginning, Baccarat has always striven to manufacture crystal that would satisfy the demanding criteria of the top end of the market – heads of state, monarchs, the *crème de la crème* of the aristocracy, commerce and industry.

The tinkling of breaking crystal is often heard in the works. Any item that is flawed in any way and fails any of the numerous stringent quality control checks is ruthlessly destroyed. Crystal-making is no sinecure and nearly 40 per cent of the output, most looking perfectly good and highly desirable to the average eye, is carried back to the melting pot to be recycled.

Not surprisingly, crystal dominates the tidy prosperous-looking town of Baccarat. Every second shop seems to be in the business of selling crystal, some of it 'Not The Real Thing' and imported. The glassworks, in turn, preside over everything and the company employs around 1,100 skilled artisans, many of them living on the premises in houses belonging to Baccarat.

In the 'hot' phase of the crystal-making one of the workshops is equipped with a huge roaring circular beehive of a furnace. From its twenty mouths, known as 'pots', the molten red crystal is collected on the tip of blowpipes. Teams of glass-blowers then fashion the glowing mixture of silica, lead oxide and potassium oxide into well-nigh perfect pieces. Here as in Biot – but on

*Left* Glassmaker's cottage. In the old days a bell would call people to work at odd hours day and night. Seventy or so families were housed on the premises. The times are different and the work organized in normal shifts but many employees have opted to live in the cottages.

*Opposite* These tiny pearls are segments from rods of coloured glass. They will be enclosed in a smooth casing of solid crystal to make the popular millefiori paperweights (*far right*). *Millefiori* – literally thousand flowers – were a popular design in the 19th Century. The technique originated in the glass works of Venice during the Renaissance.

*Opposite below left* Crystal earrings from Baccarat. *Opposite below right* 'Diva', a vase designed for Baccarat in 1990 by Nicolas Tribouletin.

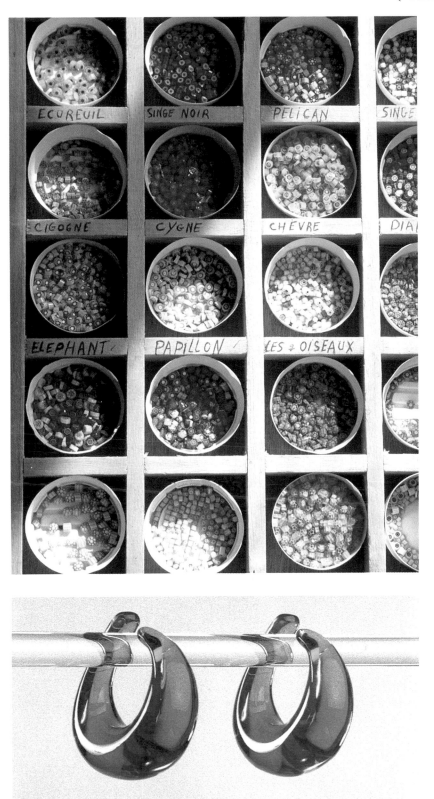

a much larger and more complex scale – the dance of the glass-workers is intricate and mysterious.

For this ambitious ballet the corps has many members: some of the bigger pieces are worked on by a team of ten or twelve artisans. To the head of the team go the most skilled jobs, such as applying stems or handles, something which requires years of expertise, perfect visual judgement and great precision. The men need strength as well as dexterity: containing 30 per cent lead (crystal is a glass which contains at least 24 per cent lead oxide), Baccarat crystal is very heavy. The lead also helps make it totally clear and vibrantly resonant.

After the hot house the crystal goes to cooling ovens where it will be allowed to lose heat very gradually, to avoid strain. After more thorough checks, the 'cold working' starts. The painstaking processes of cutting and engraving bring out the brilliance and light-reflecting qualities of crystal. At this stage, as earlier in the hot house, the artisans working on the glass are consummate masters of their crafts. Between fifteen and twenty of them hold the coveted title of *Un des Meilleurs Ouvriers de France* (One of the Best Workmen of France) awarded every three to four years to the most skilled artisans in various disciplines (see page 104).

Cutting is done by different kinds of wheels, with the cutter working like a sculptor, using his eyes and his hands to create precise facets and patterns. Engraved decorations are executed with tiny wheels, or by stencilling motifs with special ink on to the crystal which is then later bathed in slightly corrosive hydrofluoric acid. Sometimes gold is brushed on and the piece heated again to make it adhere.

Although the Baccarat works are not open to the general public, visitors to the town from Easter through the summer months can see the crystal collections at the museum in the *château*, the large house built in the park close to the works nearly two hundred years ago to receive distinguished clients. In gently creaky rooms with fine wood panels, grand glittering displays await: opalines, historic table services, glasses and astonishing paperweights. The round millefiori paperweights, in particular, are made of over 100 tiny different canes of coloured glass. Arranged in an exquisite pattern, they are covered by a smooth top layer of crystal. A range of tools and documents also give an idea of how the crystal is made and worked. From millefiori paperweights to classic glasses and vases, from stunningly simple crystal earrings to very contemporary creations by resolutely modern resident designers, the luxurious panoply of the Baccarat range is on show in the shop.

If Lorraine does not feature on your itinerary, next time you are in Paris take the opportunity to visit the Baccarat Museum. Located at 30 rue de Paradis, in the busy heart of the old glass and china district near the Gare de l'Est, it is larger than its Vosges counterpart and sparkles with innumerable pieces of crystal, some two hundred years old. Candelabra designed for the Shah of Persia and the Russian Czarina, dozens of chandeliers, ornate precious vases for nabobs and maharajahs, decanters, *coupes* and stemmed glasses glimmer everywhere you look. Housed in glass cabinets is a unique collection of perfume bottles, designed for the great *parfumeurs* of Paris, some looking delightfully absurd and decadent with their jaunty little stoppers.

## FROM CRAFT TO ART: A FAMILY PASSION

When his family's textile business seemed on the brink of collapse in 1969, engineer Claude Morin decided to begin a new working life as a glass-maker. With a young family to support, some friends thought Morin's change of direction something of a gamble, but his wife Florence was equally enthusiastic. Inspired by the work of ceramicist and glass-maker Etienne Noël in Dieulefit, Morin was further convinced by a visit to Eloi Monod at Biot that his project was feasible and a realistic commercial proposition.

Classical in its inspiration, a recent glass sculpture by Claude Morin.

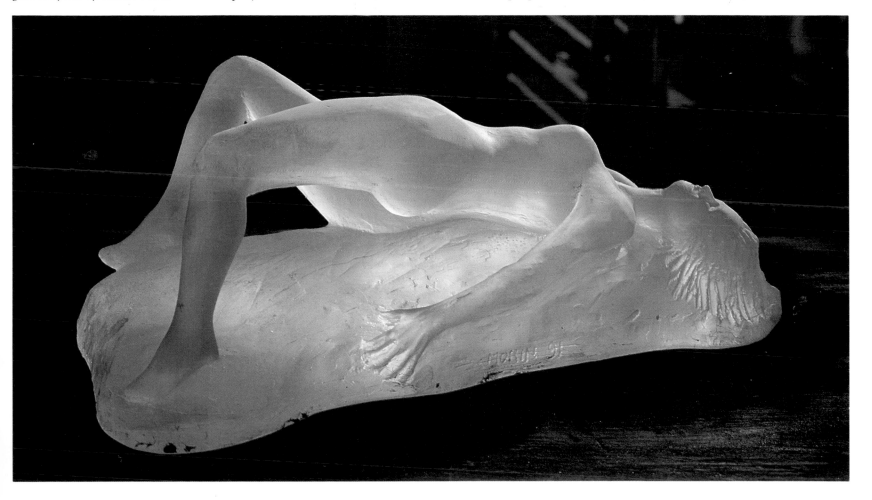

Architectural sculpture in glass, metal and light by Frédéric Morin (*left*) and vase by Nicolas Morin (*right*). Where does craft end and art begin? There is no easy answer. Contemporary glass-blowers like Claude Morin and his sons Nicolas and Frédéric may be creating works of art but they are the first to insist that in order to achieve this, they had to master every aspect of the ancient craft of glass-making. Behind the gallery where their work is exhibited in Dieulefit is an extraordinary workshop in which father and sons go on experimenting with glass and its myriad possibilities.

*Vase Croco* by Nicolas Morin. Nicolas has recently been working on a series of 'crocodile vases' in which he uses a number of complex techniques to create very contemporary glass pieces.

Never having held a blowpipe before, he learned in a hurry, and the studio opened in 1970, housed in an old Dieulefit factory. Morin's engineering background and fascination with solving technical problems soon resulted in a made-to-measure workshop, equipped with inventions and gadgets designed to make the born-again solo glass-maker's life easier. Cooling curtains of water, furnace and oven doors activated by foot-pedals, and ventilators were all admired (and sometimes copied) by visitors. They were also much appreciated by Claude and by his elder sons, Frédéric and Nicolas, who soon joined their father in the studio during school holidays.

Dieulefit, 30 kilometres (19 miles) east of Montélimar and celebrated for its ceramics and pottery, has always been a popular destination attracting large numbers of regular visitors. Morin's business soon flourished, so much so that he eventually had to stop making some successful articles – such as the best-selling wall vases – in order to avoid becoming a production line turning out single models.

Rather than producing to meet demand, Morin wanted to create decorative but simple forms, such as pots, bottles, jars, pitchers, *coupes* and vases that could be used as well as admired. Colour techniques were also experimented with – a difficult-to-achieve bull's-blood red in particular. Over the years the studio became well-known in the glass world and leading international artists, like Harvey Littleton, Bob Fritz and Joel Myers, came and went.

Having clearly inherited the family's wide-ranging talents, while engaged in academic and other pursuits, Frédéric and Nicolas developed into skilled glass-blowers. Little by little the pieces created in the studio by Morin Père et Fils moved closer to art. Nicolas's work has been regularly exhibited in Paris and at major international art shows for several years. Frédéric, only recently working full-time in the studio, is experimenting with glass and metal creations. Claude Morin, now officially retired but still extremely busy, is fascinated by glass sculptures based on classical models.

Artists they may be, but the Morins, along with many other leading contemporary glass-blowers, are also complete masters of the necessary techniques. Unlike old masters such as Gallé who had to work within the limitations of an industrial context, they are able to craft glass single-handedly from beginning to end in true artisan tradition.

# TEXTILES, NEEDLEWORK AND LEATHER

When fabric-making moved from the cottage to the factory, when machines started to turn out metre after metre of perfectly acceptable cloth or even lace and when leather work became industrialized, the textile and leather crafts suffered a blow from which they only very partially recovered.

For a number of craftspeople the obvious survival strategy was to move 'up-market' and make bespoke luxury their unique selling proposition. In this process many artisans went – as it were – underground. They became invisible, absorbed in the workshops of the luxury goods industry – *les produits de luxe*. Even if not actually employed on the premises, many people work on contract from home exclusively for one client. For the casually interested customer, finding the addresses of these well-hidden artisans – and getting them to make something – is far from easy.

Others have made a virtue of necessity and kept their threatened craft alive by marketing it as a hobby craft. They make a living by teaching their skills to people who have no intention of becoming a professional lace-maker or embroiderer. The customers, in this case, will buy the necessary paraphernalia and expertise from the artisan and perhaps a few samples of excellent work. They are keen to learn a satisfying leisure activity and they take it extremely seriously. Lace-making (see page 116) is probably the most striking example of a rejuvenated craft.

Another survival tactic is to turn an old hand-craft into a labour-intensive light industry. The trick here is to hit a happy balance between the two, to produce articles that have neither the look nor feel of something mass-produced but which may be afforded by a reasonable number of customers. The cloth printers of Provence (see page 129), for instance, have been doing this with great success for some time.

Once an outworker's poorly paid toil, now a hobbyist labour of love, lace-making has made a comeback.

## THE DELICATE ART OF LACE-MAKING

Some three decades ago, at the dawning of the age of the computer, any sensible person drawing up a list of the traditional crafts that seemed most unlikely to survive in France would very probably have included lace-making. In commercial terms, it never was a good way to earn a living. It takes a good lace-maker one entire day to work a one centimetre piece of intricate lace ten centimetres wide.

Up until the beginning of this century, for many women making lace at home was an economic necessity, the best possible way of making money on a regular basis. Inevitably they were exploited and paid a pittance. In the nineteenth century a lace-maker's monthly earnings were not enough to buy a kilo (2 lb) of meat. No wonder that in many French towns the districts where lace was made were also 'red-light areas'.

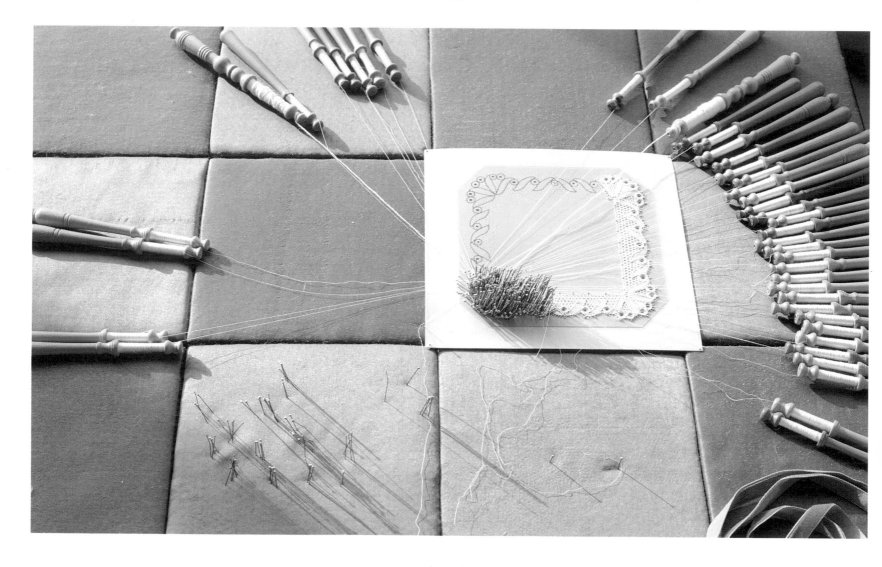

Tell a group of modern lace-makers – happily beavering away with their bobbins and pins – that their predecessors had to turn to prostitution to make ends meet, and the chances are they will smile or laugh politely. If they spend hour after hour labouring over a tiny area of fine linen these days it is entirely by choice, because they enjoy it and get great satisfaction from their work.

Lace-making has, by and large, become a hobby craft. The professionals, the highly skilled women who keep the traditions alive, often earn part of their living as instructors, teaching the techniques to enthusiastic students who want to take up lace-making in their leisure hours.

Of course the professional *dentellières* complain about money, but no more than you'd expect. All the ones I met were totally committed to their chosen work. They also seem to have succeeded in making converts: doomed in conventional commercial terms, lace-making is thriving as a hobby craft, with a large and passionate international following. Clubs and associations, avidly read newsletters and magazines, regular meetings, classes, the exchange of patterns and tips… the lace-making sorority is a closely knit network.

I use the word sorority because this tends to be a female pastime, although not exclusively. I was told of a retired pastry chef by the name of Jean-Pierre who used to chauffeur his wife Micheline to her lace lessons twice a week. He got bored with patiently waiting in the car or in the café while the bobbins clicked away, so he too enrolled. Perhaps it is because *pâtissiers* tend to have deft fingers, but Jean-Pierre (who by the sound of it had fast become teacher's pet) soon caught up with his wife and is now a skilled lace-maker.

In France, lace-making centres are scattered all over the country: from Quimper in Brittany to the Vosges, and from the north to the Auvergne. While Calais is the leading French producer of industrial lace, in Valenciennes – home of the *cheveu d'ange*, the delicate 'angel hair' lace – and in Bailleul, the traditional skills originally inspired by the lace of Flanders are still going strong. Gone are the days when you used to see an old lady making lace in every second house of Le Puy, but the town has remained an important venue, with the Centre d'Initiation à la Dentelle du Puy acting as a national school, showroom and shop. Also in the Auvergne, north-west of Le Puy and overlooking the Allier river, the city of Brioude is as famed for its lace as it once was for its iron works.

Needle lace is alive and well in the Vosges, in the spa town of Luxeuil. However, the Normandy city of Alençon is really the spiritual home of this craft. It was in Alençon that Colbert, Louis XIV's enormously influential trade minister, opened the Manufacture Royale du Point de France to give birth to France's *appellation contrôlée* lace. Arachnidean and exquisitely fine, it soon became part of the country's national heritage and still enjoys government support to this day. Indeed the Atelier National du Point d'Alençon came under the aegis of the Ministry of Culture in 1976.

Not far from Alençon in Argentan, intricate needle-linen lace with a

Waiting for deft fingers to resume their work: A lace-maker's pillow with innumerable pins and dozens of bobbins, all neatly arranged.

delicate hexagonal ground is still being made by Benedictine nuns. Visitors are welcomed into the showroom to admire and buy the community's work.

To get an informative, lively introduction to lace-making by enthusiastic and well-organized professionals, a good place to visit is Bayeux. There – quite properly close to the Cathedral with its lacy stonework – in a fine peaceful town house that was once the home of the local bishop, you will find the Conservatoire de la Dentelle de Bayeux. Lace-making had been very much a traditional local activity for hundreds of years. A century ago, the old

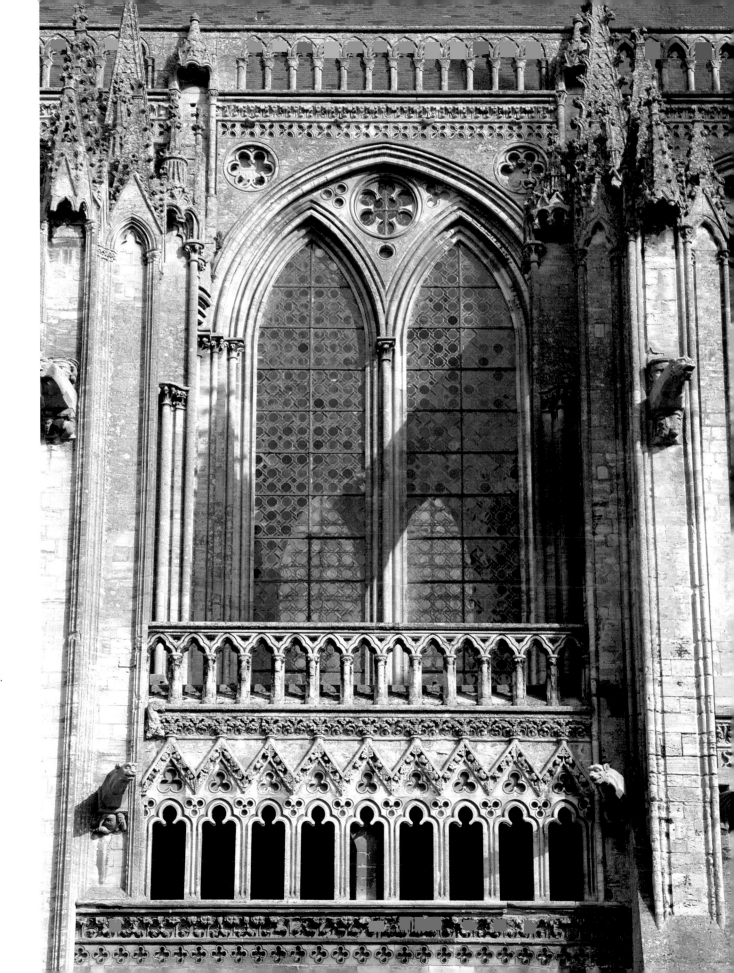

Bayeux Cathedral, with its
gloriously ornate lacy stonework.

A lace-maker at work. When making bobbin lace the basic movement is cross and twist, *croiser, tourner*. Beginners are encouraged to repeat the words to themselves rather like a mantra until they get the right rhythm going. A very detailed cartoon fixed on the pillow is always used as a guide.

town was the centre of a lace revival. All the various types of lace started to be made in Bayeux, including the popular black chantilly lace.

In the days when hoops and shawls were fashionable, there were 5,000 women in Bayeux (and 50,000 in Normandy) busily making the pieces of lace, *les mesles*, that would be assembled by a seamstress known as the *raboutisseuse* (the needle-woman-who-joins-up). The last hoop of a dress was 12 metres (40 ft) wide and 30 cm (1 ft) high while a large shawl was made of anything up to twenty pieces and involved the work of twenty lace-makers, so there was work for all.

By the mid-Seventies, however, when economics graduate Marie-Hélène Salvador began to research Bayeux lace, there was little left. The tradition was a purely oral one, and only a handful of lace-makers was still working. So she set to work methodically reading old documents, examining old lace with the help of magnifying glasses and micro-photography while becoming skilled enough in her own right to be awarded France's top craft qualification, the Meilleur Ouvrier de France medal.

Mylène (short for Marie-Hélène) was soon joined by a trio of fellow enthusiasts, Sylvie Malard, Florence Quinette and Fabienne Ros, and all four have been busy ever since, not just with their bobbins but also promoting, teaching and selling Bayeux lace. They have enjoyed some degree of official support: perhaps more than any other region in France, Normandy seems to excel at keeping alive and marketing its traditional heritage. Bayeux has been no exception. Impressed by one of their lace-making demonstrations, the Mayor helped Mylène and her colleagues find the Conservatoire its present spacious home and the council assists with an all-important regular subsidy.

The Conservatoire teaches around eighty students on a weekly four-hour basis and runs short introductory courses. As well as authenticating and valuing old lace, its many other activities include organizing exhibitions and well-attended international lace conferences (over a hundred lace-makers – mostly from the USA, Quebec, Holland, Belgium and Great Britain – took part in the last biannual event).

Visitors to the peaceful airy house will see Mylène, with her colleagues and students, at work on cartoons fixed on pretty round pillows spiked with pins on which rest dozens of bobbins. Hands flicker and the bobbins cross and turn the fine thread of linen or silk in mysterious yet clearly regular and precise ways – a totally absorbing spectacle for a first-time visitor. Making visitors aware of the work that is being done is very much part of the Conservatoire's approach. The next step is to reassure would-be students that lace-making very quickly turns into an enjoyable and satisfying activity, even if you never get close to mastering the 135 or so different stitches.

After a few hours' work you can start making simple but pretty things. After twenty hours or so, you can begin to mix and match stitches and embark on making napkins and the like. Lace-making is a popular option with the

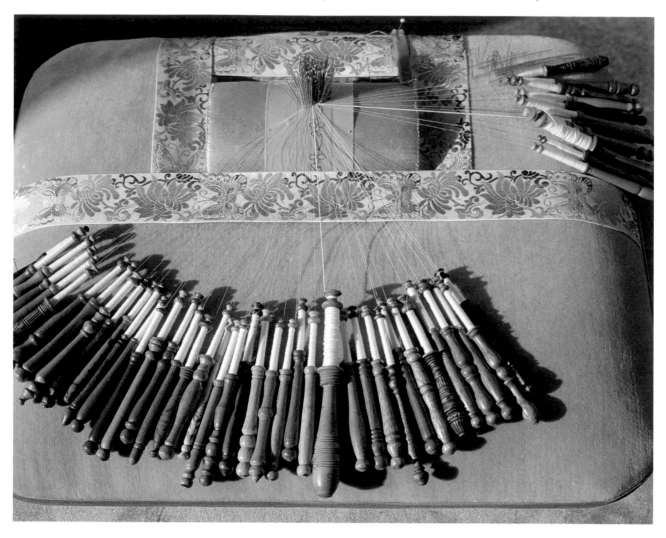

Like everything to do with lace-making, the tools of the trade are pretty and feminine. More often than not, pillows and bobbins are decorated. The bobbins in particular tend to be extremely ornate and their shape can vary a great deal from region to region.

schoolgirls of Bayeux. In an effort to make yet one more new convert, Fabienne Ros encouragingly showed me the work of seven-year-olds. 'Why not give it a try? You'll be hooked, you'll see...' I was impressed by the work and tempted by the bobbins, but hard-earned knowledge of my limitations made me turn down the offer.

The time had clearly come to go into the shop and showroom to admire the lace on display. Medallions, initials, page-markers, napkins, collars and handkerchiefs all looked pristine and exquisite in their glass cases. I particularly liked the discreet collars and the delightful sew-on initials. They looked fragile, but apparently this was deceptive. Hand-made lace lasts much longer and continues to look better than its machine-woven poor coarse relative. Lace is expensive and therefore smaller pieces are much easier to sell to those discriminating first-time buyers who are aware of the difference between real lace and industrial lace.

Much of the work is commissioned, clients often ordering personalized pieces. The Conservatoire's favoured customers tend to be people for whom lace is a case of love-at-first-sight. They cannot resist the appeal of lace and buy a piece as they would a watercolour or work of art. Particularly 'susceptible', apparently, are visitors from the USA and Canada.

The biggest and most prestigious order to date was commissioned by the town of Bayeux to commemorate the Prince and Princess of Wales's visit in 1987 as part of the William the Conqueror anniversary year. What has since entered into the town's history and is referred to casually but with pride as *l'éventail de Lady Di,* Princess Diana's fan, took over a thousand hours of work to make – a less conservative estimate is fifteen hundred. The choice of a fan as a gift fit for a royal visitor was Mylène Salvador's suggestion as a result of her research. Soon she found herself playing – at any given time – with some six hundred bobbins on her pillow. Sylvie Malard, another Meilleur Ouvrier de France, created the original cartoon, showing – on a floral ground – a viking ship, William the Conqueror as King, and the English crown. Before the unique fan left Bayeux forever it was on show for several weeks and the inhabitants of the town had a chance to admire the present to which they firmly refuse to ascribe a price.

What of the future? There aren't quite enough princesses around to guarantee regular large commissions... quite realistically the lace-makers at the Conservatoire do not really recommend their craft as an ideal full-time occupation for a girl – but as a gratifying hobby, yes, definitely. The situation is much better than it was in the very early days of the Conservatoire some fifteen years ago. The international sorority of lace-makers is interested in the work carried out in Bayeux and meetings are well attended; tourists flock to visit the workshop and many buy something. Although there will never be more than a handful of people willing to train professionally, there are enough advanced students (and little girls getting hooked at an early age) to guarantee that the old tradition will survive.

Two pieces of work by Conservatoire students. Progress is slow, and labour-intensive lace is measured in centimetres.

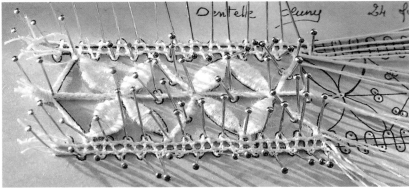

*Left* A weaver at work: Michèle Cosnier at her loom, one of two taking up much of the space in her small workshop.

*Opposite* A traditional Normandy drugget skirt made by Michèle Cosnier for a folk-dance group.

## A DEDICATED WEAVER

One of Mylène Salvador's regular students at the Bayeux Lace Conservatoire is Michèle Cosnier. She attends sessions out of professional interest in order to be able, in turn, to answer questions and explain lace-making to visitors, clients and students. For Michèle is a textile expert in her own right, a rare representative of a fast-disappearing *artisanat*, the weaver working from home. The current weaving business being what it is, she has to be ready to diversify on occasion.

Less than one hundred years ago in the part of Normandy where Mademoiselle Cosnier lives, near Domfront and la Ferté-Macé in the Orne – the heart of the green *bocage,* the characteristic hedged pastures intermingled with woodland of the region – there used to be around 50,000 weavers working at home. This was often in the cellar of the house, a room with a low ceiling and small windows separated from the living quarters by an external staircase. The weaver was a linchpin in the local economy, this cottage industry keeping a small group of people in work. Until the advent of cotton, hemp was grown, soaked and treated in Normandy as in many parts of France. The flax was spun and the threads brought to the weaver.

Each village had its traditional designs – clothing probably even more markedly then than now being used to distinguish the wearer, to tell others where a person came from and denote his or her status. Within the same

Centuries-old samples of *droguet*, the cloth of Normandy. Like many others passionate about their craft Michèle Cosnier has a strong sense of local history and a collector's instinct for interesting artefacts. Swatches such as these help her re-create authentic woven cloth. In the old days drugget patterns varied from village to village and people could distinguish each other at a glance by their clothes.

social class, costumes varied subtly from region to region, details changing a little from village to village. Dress was ritually different on religious festivals, high-days and holidays.

The old order changed quickly with the arrival of cotton. Instead of being a local crop, cotton tended to be supplied to the home-weaver, often with loom and equipment. Pressure was put on artisans to come and work in factories where their output would be more steady than at home where they also worked in the fields. Weaving invariably came to a stop at harvest time and other crucial dates in the agricultural calendar. The advent of cotton marked the beginning of the end for the old cottage weaving industry.

In her grey granite cottage near the church in Dompierre, a village which bursts with heaps of blue hydrangeas in the summer months but looks somewhat more severe for the rest of the year, Michèle Cosnier weaves the traditional cloth of Normandy, the *droguet*. The old French word has made its way into English as 'drugget' – the kind of word crossword enthusiasts enjoy toying with. Chambers Dictionary defines drugget as a woven and felted coarse woollen fabric.

*Droguet* apparently loses a great deal in translation. The fabric that emerges from Michèle's loom is anything but coarse. It is a closely woven mixture of linen warp and wool weft, pleasantly hard to the touch, with a good heavy feel and very tight texture. Its colours vary a great deal: a lot of blue, brick-red, off-white, some yellow, very little brown. The samples and pieces of material in Michèle's workshop were mostly striped with tints that seemed to have come straight down from the Bayeux tapestry.

With the exception of a few attractive shawls and other pieces made for the relatively light passing trade – this part of the Orne is not on the main Normandy tourist beat – Michele's work is mostly commissioned. Her principal customers have been *groupes folkloriques*, country dancing groups, intent on donning the genuine old costumes of Normandy when they perform. They bring her worn-out garments, pictures, pieces of material which she uses as reference. Much time is also spent in museums and antique shops researching the history of local costumes and textiles. Word of her activities has gotten around and complete strangers who have heard of her work send her ancient fabric swatches and documents. One real problem is finding wools that adequately match the subtle colours of the old vegetable dyes. Michèle has discovered a Swedish supplier whose range of tints passes her stringent test. Unfortunately, the wools are extremely expensive.

The high costs involved explain why so few individual weavers are still sitting at their looms. Take an 'ordinary' drugget skirt. Worn with a white shirt, a little jerkin or short-sleeved jacket, white stockings, pumps and Normandy head-dress, it is standard attire for folk country dancing. The traditional skirt is very full and needs to be made up of 3 metres (10 ft) of material. For each individual skirt, commissioned to match the customer's chosen design, the loom first has to be set up. All 1,100 warp threads have to be patiently put into place one by one – there are ten threads per centimetre ($\frac{1}{3}$ in) and, allowing for a little shrinkage, the width of the finished drugget will be just over one metre (40 in). The complex and careful threading takes well over a day.

Next comes the weaving – a metre represents a good hard day's work, with interruptions when a thread breaks or a mistake (hard to rectify later) is spotted. Concentration is required, but a working rhythm soon gets going and Michèle can often have the radio playing in the background over the rather disjointed noise of the loom. A man's job in the old days, weaving is not a soft comfortable occupation: after weaving a metre of cloth Michèle feels tired and achy in the evening.

With setting up the loom and three solid days' weaving, all in all it takes the best part of a week to produce enough drugget to make a dancing skirt. Michèle's margins are more than modest but, once the costs of the wool and linen are included, the price to the customer has to be high. If people understand the work that goes into weaving a unique piece of material, they are happy to pay for it. Others – and they are in the majority – just cannot appreciate the difference in quality.

The other commercial snag is that *droguet* simply never wears out. With its close texture and strong fibres, it was meant to give a lifetime's wear, gradually felting and fading a little. How did people clean their *droguet* clothes? Not very often, Michèle thinks. Perhaps they brought it once a year to the fuller's mill to flush out the accumulated dirt with the help of earth and water.

Allow me to digress for a moment and issue a word of warning. Intrigued by Mademoiselle Cosnier's description of the fuller's mills, I noticed a signposted Route des Moulins circuit near Caen and persuaded Hugh Palmer that it would offer unique photo opportunities. Unfortunately, this was not the case. Every mill seemed to have been relocated, *à la* old London Bridge. We meandered pleasantly but unsuccessfully and have yet to see – let alone photograph – a Normandy fuller's mill.

Michèle's customers tend to take their skirts to the local dry cleaners rather than the mill, but they too do not go in for repeat orders. A skirt will serve them well until their dancing days are over. I never actually wore a *droguet* skirt myself, even at the height of my so-called dancing days, but I could think of lots of ways of using the quietly beautiful pieces of fabric Michele showed me, with their subtle stripes or bands and harmonious colours.

# FROM INDIA TO PROVENCE

Perhaps because France's relatively short-lived – and not particularly intense – involvement with the Indian sub-continent took place in the age of elegance and at a time when the known world was still thought to hold in store romantic wonders, the adjective *indienne* is still redolent of tempered exoticism. When not describing a mildly fragrant chicken dish, it usually refers to the printed floral cloths that gradually made their appearance on ships bound home from the East at the end of the seventeenth century. The materials. similar to British paisley, soon became so popular with fashionable people that Louis XV, true to the French commercial ethos, banned them from being imported in an effort to protect the French home market.

The ancient Indian and Persian techniques of printing and colouring cloth – originally with stencils and later with hand blocks – were adopted with enthusiasm in Provence during the eighteenth century. Strong colours had always been popular in the region – the red of the madder, the blue of the indigo plant, the yellow extracted from the sap of various vegetables – as had floral and pastoral motifs. Tints and designs lent themselves well to the newly acquired techniques. The huge shawls and the head scarves that had always been part of the costume of local women and the brightly printed cottons that were used in every Provençal home became synonymous with Provence... *le Style Provençal* was born.

With their earthy sun-drenched colours and their vivid patterns, the printed cottons of Provence are a joy to behold.

Vegetable dyes and old wood hand-blocks (*below*) are no longer used, but colours and patterns remain unchanged (*right*).

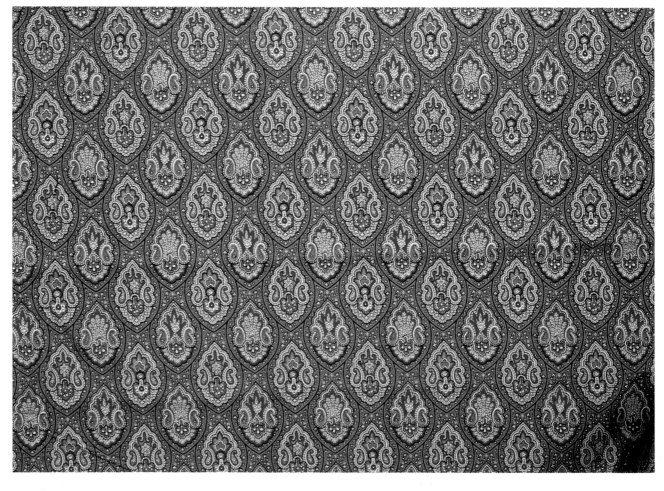

Leaving Valence and heading north-east towards Romans-sur-Isère, you may just drive past a couple of discreet shop windows. If you happen to catch a glimpse of clear sunny colours, you may well decide that the shop is worth a stop and your instinct will be right. You are at the home of Valdrôme, specialists in Provençal prints since 1946 and the modern incarnation of a very old local print industry. The shop is a genuine treasure-house of Provençal materials. It is completely unpretentious, with old-fashioned shelves and display baskets crammed high with rolls of cotton, clothes, quilted bags, table sets, tablecloths, napkins, shawls, scarves, boxes, braids and rugs. Everywhere you look, you see a tempting heap of colours and patterns. Pull out a roll of cloth, then another catches your eye, and another... it is impossible not to be distracted. I did eventually manage to tear myself away to go backstage, as it were, to find out more about Valdrôme and the Provençal print tradition.

Vegetable dyestuffs and hand blocks have long been abandoned in order to make materials not only affordable but also easier to wash. Modern inks are used which can stand high temperatures without running – in fact they come out better if washed at over 60°C (140°F). What matters, and what a great deal of effort goes into, is to be able to recreate on a regular basis the true bold colours of Provence – black, red, yellow, blue and brick – and to come as close as possible to the shades of the old vegetable dyestuffs. A collection of old hand blocks is used to reproduce the motifs and designs of the past. The same colours and the same designs have been popular year after year, ever since Valdrôme started just after the war. This is not the land of pastels or monochromes and to its many fans the Provençal style remains outside fashion, never dating and therefore never needing to change.

The basic material is top-quality cotton imported from China, the world's major cotton producer. The bales are bleached and mercerized in France to uniform standards in order to ensure an even quality. The great, treated rolls – they are 500 metres (just under one-third of a mile) long – then go to Valdrôme's printers. An average of six colours are used, but several popular designs incorporate eight or more. Printing techniques vary: in some cases, in a process known as discharge dyeing, bleaches wash out the dyes in gradual stages, the lighter background emerging at the end; in another process, the fine lines of the motif, the hardest to position on the cloth, are coloured first and the ground is then filled in one colour at a time. The whole length (50 metres/55 yards) and width (1.5 or 1.8 metres/5 or 6 ft) of the printed cotton rolls are all individually examined on Valdrôme's checking machines for register and overall quality.

Then comes the cutting, which takes place in spacious light workshops on the first floor of the same house as the shop. Even the patterns hanging on the wall are made of brightly coloured card. Pieces are all hand-cut, scissors whooshing against cloth. Braids which are printed in 1.5 metre (5 ft) widths like the rest, are sliced as unceremoniously as salami. For each garment, bag

*Overleaf* Printing the six (or sometimes eight colours) of Provençal cloth is done in several stages. Often the pattern comes first, then the colours are added one at a time.

Lightly padded with cotton wadding, a piece of yellow cloth is being cut to make a bright spectacles case.

*Left and right* Brightly coloured
quilted place mats from Provence.

A collection of brightly-coloured, warm-looking shawls.

or accessory, the various pieces are gathered in a neat little bundle and tied together with multicoloured off-cuts.

The articles then get machined and hand-finished on the premises. Sometimes they are dispatched to out-workers for assembling and stitching. As I was standing in the workshop, one woman came in with a batch of garments, clutching her car keys, sorry that she couldn't stay to have a chat but she had to pick up the kids from school.

Another traditional line is quilted cotton, which is used for making rugs, bags, pouches, purses, and for Valdrôme's best selling line – table sets. The quilted printed cotton is backed with a fine tight cotton wadding and lined with a plain cotton that matches the dominant colour of the print. Despite its casually elegant appearance, it too is very robust and thrives on being washed at high temperatures.

The celebrated *indienne* shawls and scarves, with such a glorious history, are made of fine wool serge with a diagonal weave and impeccable colours. As light as they are warm, they give perfect protection against the great hazard of the otherwise mellow climate, the persistent chilling gusts of cold north wind known as the Mistral that so often blows down the Rhone valley. After seeing them at Valdrôme, I could not stop noticing *indienne* shawls on the shoulders of Provençal women everywhere I went.

However, Valdrôme's pride and joy and the most truly artisanal of the company's products are their luxurious huge mohair shawls. Hand-woven and extremely light but very dense, they are tricky to print. The process is done by hand on flat frames and each of the twelve colours of any shawl needs to be gone over no fewer than fourteen times.

## EMBROIDERY AND TAPESTRY

Just as lace-making has survived to enjoy yet another new lease of life as a hobby craft, so too has embroidery – perhaps even more so, I was told by Marie-Catherine Nobécourt who teaches both crafts at the Atelier de l'Horloge in Bayeux. She went on to explain that the reason for this extraordinary popularity is that many men are quite happy to take up embroidery as a calming, soothing pastime. In fact, the craft is acquiring quite a new following. I did seem to recall a number of French male media personalities – from actors to food critics – happy to be photographed relaxing with their embroidery frames, needles and threads.

As a commercial proposition, the skill of hand-embroidery has perhaps survived better in France than in most other countries, largely thanks to Paris *haute couture*. Several small businesses and many individuals still work discreetly and exclusively to order for the luxury end of the fashion trade. Many of them are Paris-based. Intricate embroidery – just like lace-making – does not come cheap.

If you are interested in taking up embroidery as a hobby craft, Mademoiselle Nobécourt will eloquently persuade you that the best and easiest way to start is to master the stitch of Bayeux. It is named after the original, one-and-only surviving work embroidered in this way towards the end of the eleventh century, the Bayeux Tapestry. For that most famous of all medieval 'tapestries' was, in fact, embroidered rather than woven on lengths of linen material.

The tapestry dominates the town of Bayeux. The original itself, in its long glass cabinet, more than lives up to any expectations you may have. It manages to be both uniquely absorbing and moving, still fresh and lively after over nine hundred years, despite the long queues of visitors, the surfeit of audio-visual aids and the difficulty of walking in time with the headphone commentary. In the town, it quickly becomes too much of a good thing. Every souvenir shop, every second restaurant, *pâtisserie* and car park seem to be named after the Tapisserie or after Guillaume, its hero William the Conqueror, and William's wife, Queen Mathilda, la Reine Mathilde. Indeed, in French the tapestry itself is usually referred to as *la Tapisserie de la Reine Mathilde*, Queen Mathilda's tapestry.

That Mathilda herself had a hand in embroidering the tapestry is more than extremely unlikely. Mademoiselle Nobécourt, who has spent many years researching medieval tapestries and epic sagas – from Iceland to Provence – estimates that it would take a team of five proficient embroiderers working half-time (as the original people must have done in the short daylight hours all those centuries ago) at least four and a half years to embroider a panel of that size, 70 metres (230 feet) long.

The embroiderers in the medieval workshop used wool which had been tinted with vegetable dyes. The colours of muted brick, rust, mustard yellow, olive-green, dark brown and off-white are also found in cloth traditionally woven in the region (see page 124 *ff*). In the stitch of Bayeux, the linen cloth is left bare as a background and the fine wool designs are then embroidered to stand out distinctively.

First a forward outline stitch is used to surround the design. Then a different colour thread is used to fill the design in three steps: tight parallel threads are stitched over the material, then perpendicular threads are stretched on top, a few millimetres from each other; finally much smaller stitches, sometimes in a different colour, fix the perpendicular lines to the cloth at regular intervals.

As well as cameos reproducing scenes and motifs from the tapestry – such as the Ploughman, the Hand of God, Harold with his pack of dogs, William's long ship – embroidered tapestries on display and for sale at the Atelier de l'Horloge include delightful medieval samplers, alphabets and animals. Embroidery kits, complete with linen cloth, wool threads and full instructions are also available.

A segment of the Bayeux Tapestry showing William Duke of Normandy sitting in splendour in Bayeux. Not shown is the treacherous Harold swearing fealty to his Lord with his hands not just on one but on two holy reliquaries … Only close examination will show that this evocative scene is not a fragment of the original Tapestry but a faithful cameo embroidered in the Atelier de l'Horloge.

An old watermill not far from the Atelier de l'Horloge. Bayeux is a compact place with delightful visual surprises at many of its street corners. A good time to discover the town is in early spring or late autumn when it has a slightly melancholy off-season atmosphere and is relatively free of visitors.

If you want to try your hand at this therapeutic hobby, whether only for one quick introductory session or for one full year, you can enrol as a student. Mademoiselle Nobécourt and her colleagues teach embroidery as well as lace-making throughout the year. She sees the few modern professionals of embroidery very much as teachers 'instructing people who have time to spare in old skills and techniques that will enrich their lives, rather than trying to train newcomers to do a job that no longer really exists in commercial terms.'

Hanging on a wall in the workshop, pieces of leather, harnesses and other paraphernalia.

## THE HOME OF HAND-MADE SADDLES

Gone are the days when leather used to be worked at a craft level in villages throughout the French countryside. Even so, if you look very hard and if luck is on your side during your travels, you may still be able to find old-style galoshes in Brittany, traditional gloves in Millau and possibly the odd bag or satchel here and there.

Hand-made leather goods have become luxury items. The artisans who produce them tend to work for the *crème de la crème* of Paris boutiques and stores. For instance, Hermès – the most prestigious of all – employs well over two hundred highly skilled leather workers in its workshops. Many more craftsmen operate from their own premises as regular exclusive out-workers.

Setting up on your own as a leather artisan is practically impossible, Bruno Pottier told me when I visited his workshop and boutique in Saumur. Monsieur Pottier knows what he is talking about. He is one of the very few

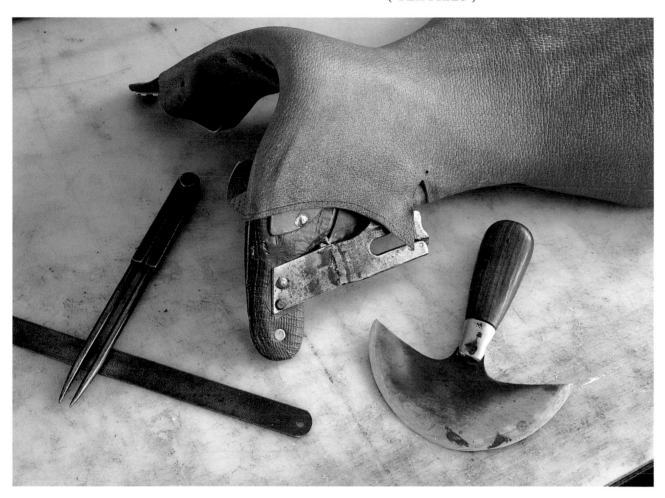

*Left* The tools of the trade, polished and a little worn with age.

*Below* In Bruno Pottier's saddles the stitching is invisible.

men in France – and also in Europe – who makes saddles by hand from start to finish.

First of all it takes ten years to become truly skilled and to master all the tricks and fine points of leather work. Then, since the articles you will be making will be expensive and of interest to only a very limited number of potential customers, you will have the considerable problem of building up your clientele. The odds are certainly stacked against newcomers in this business.

Bruno Pottier reckons he would never have been able to do what he is doing now if he hadn't taken on the business, workshop and clientele from his father, Daniel. A master saddle-maker who had perfected his skills working at Hermès, Monsieur Pottier Père set up shop in Saumur, home of the French equestrian tradition and a very good place for a gifted artisan to create and build up his client list.

The Pottiers' reputation as the very best of French saddle-makers had somehow reached even my non-horsey ears. Seeing two or three very

Saddles leave the workshop with an impeccably smooth finish and a deep natural sheen. This is achieved by carefully buffing the leather with a piece of warmed wood.

*Right* A corner of the shop where Bruno Pottier and his wife receive their customers. It is a large room well stocked with riding gear and accessories including this handsome red saddle.

*Below* Stitching is done with two long needles and requires surgical precision.

Smoothing out any rough edges on a leather strap.

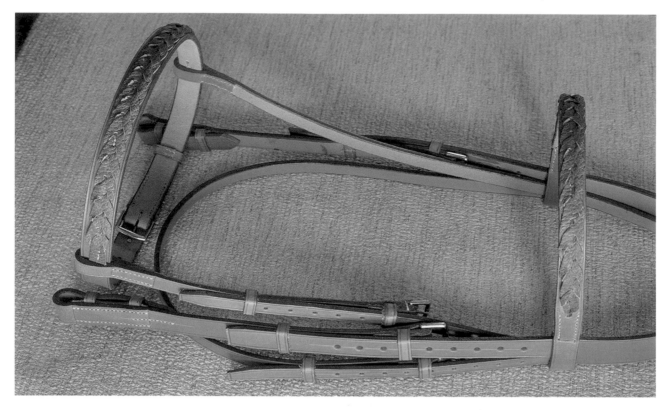

A harness fit for a noble heart.

A bespoke pigskin satchel. In addition to saddles and harnesses, Bruno Pottier occasionally makes other leather goods – all to order and when time allows. Customers have to be prepared to wait.

distinguished representatives of the French riding elite, straight-backed and elegantly formal, walking casually into the shop rather as I do into my regular local booksellers, convinced me that I was in the right place.

Nobody seemed in a hurry, neither Monsieur le Marquis wanting an article to be repaired nor Bruno Pottier himself to deliver orders. It takes around 50 hours of work to fashion and stitch a saddle, and Bruno makes only about 25 a year – all to order and all 100 per cent by hand. Customers have to wait the best part of a year for their saddle, but they know it will give them so much pleasure every time it is used that it is uniquely worth waiting for.

Bruno's saddles, with their invisible stitching, gleaming accessories and fine sheen, are beautiful objects and definitely not for novice or average riders. He mentioned a customer who tried his new saddle – it takes about twenty hours on horseback to wear in a saddle – and came to the modest conclusion that his horsemanship was not good enough. The saddle was just too demanding for him and he reluctantly had to part with it. I also thought that once you bought a saddle it would last you a lifetime, but Bruno explained that his saddlery clientele was very constant. Saddles need adjusting and adapting, particularly when you start riding a new horse.

He was perhaps less enthusiastic about his occasional customers, the people who order *maroquinerie*, fancy or fashion leather goods (the French word, more dignified than the English phrase, comes from *maroquin* or morocco leather, the fine goat- or sheep-skins used to make bag, belts and purses). They are all 'one-offs' and he does not mind keeping them waiting a little for their new status-symbol wallet, belt or satchel.

Bruno was working at the time on a pigskin satchel which I would dearly have loved to show off casually to friends and business acquaintances: roomy and soft, with exquisite hard-to-detect stitches and again that inimitable deep soft sheen that seems to come from within the leather. This effect is apparently called *glacé*, glazing, and is achieved not by polishing – definitely not – but by buffing the leather with a piece of heated wood (hot, but not too hot, otherwise the skin would burn and tear like paper). The tool Bruno Pottier showed me looked like a well-worn cross between a mallet and a pestle made out of boxwood.

The customer who ordered this particular article would have counted the days for four or five months before taking delivery. The price? Well, I can only say that it was surprisingly moderate in the circumstances and certainly represented a lot better value than you would expect from the shops of the Faubourg Saint-Honoré, Bond Street or Rodeo Drive – or even at your own local leather goods shop.

# BASKETS AND
# BROOMS

In the beginning was the large flat basket used for winnowing corn… The old French word *van* (better known perhaps in English in the form of 'fan', but also listed as 'van' in dictionaries, originally meaning a sieve or sifting basket) gave the word the French generally use to describe basket-work and basket-making, *la vannerie*.

Basket-making is one of the oldest crafts in the world, more ancient still than the skills of pottery or weaving. Grass, thin roots, straws, rushes, flat leaves, rattan cane and willow – any materials of a reasonable length and texture that happened to be at hand – were soon woven or plaited to make containers, roofing and mats. Various techniques suited to the basic materials available evolved quite independently of each other all over the planet.

In France, hedgerow wood was used everywhere, as were straws – rye, barley and corn. Rushes grew liberally in several parts of the country, most notably perhaps in the wide marshy spaces around the Loire estuary where they are still used very occasionally to thatch cottages. Thatched cottages, with a few rare exceptions (mostly in Normandy and also in the Ardèche where gorse is used) have by and large disappeared from the landscape – even if the word *chaumière* (literally a thatched cottage) still features all-too-frequently and rather loosely to describe humble abodes or would-be rustic commercial establishments.

Despite constant demand for fine cane seating, and for quality repair and restoration work, only very few people are able to make a living out of making *vannerie* these days. Many of these committed enthusiasts learn their trade at the one and only specialist college in the country, L'Ecole Nationale d'Osiériculture et de Vannerie at Fayl-Billot in the Champagne.

For its graduates, still much in need of 'on the job' experience, there are not that many potential employers. Some of the lucky ones may find a niche locally as the region is the busiest basket-making centre in France. Others may find employment in a milder climate further to the south-west at France's other leading *Vannerie*, the remarkable Cooperative at Villaines-les-Rochers.

Hand-made wicker linen baskets.

A view of Villaines-les-Rochers on a clear day in early Spring. The cave dwellings are still very much in evidence. The standard addition of a façade provides extra room at the front of the cave.

## THE BASKET-MAKERS OF VILLAINES-LES-ROCHERS

Villaines-les-Rochers is a small village south of Tours – in the heart of Balzac country – a few winding miles from one of the prettiest of the *châteaux* of the Loire, Azay-le-Rideau. Even in a region where castles, vineyards, gardens, farm-produced goats' cheeses and family-run restaurants beckon seductively and compete for the visitor's attention at practically every crossroads, Villaines is well worth a detour.

The old troglodyte village has several of the most intriguing cave dwellings in the area, some two or three 'storeys' high. Hewn out of the rock face millennia ago, they are clearly still inhabited, pots of cascading geraniums cosily decorating front doors and windows here and there, as they do every other French cottage and town house.

Villaines also happens to be a leading basket-work centre and the home of

A glimpse of Azay-le-Rideau behind a curtain of trees. The moated fairy tale castle is one of the finest in the region.

*Below* A young willow at the end of winter, with the sap just beginning to rise. Young it may be, but it is too old for wicker work: only one-year growths are really suitable.

Cut willow stalks are bundled and left standing outside in pits of water for several months (*above*). They are stripped of their bark in the late spring or early summer, dried and kept in dark well-aired storerooms (*right*).

one of France's oldest agricultural cooperatives, dating back to the middle of the last century. With its loamy soil and numerous small rivers, Villaines had always been a natural place to cultivate willow. The local farmworkers traditionally turned their hands to basket-weaving, growing willows in the bottom of valleys, selling their wares on markets and to merchants, passing on their skills to the next generation.

Basket-making brought in a little cash, fields, gardens, backyards and vineyards produced the rest, so the village economy was more or less self-sustaining: all the food the people of Villaines consumed, from the chickens they ate on high-days and holidays to the wine they drank, was home grown – and butcher's meat was eaten only two or three times a year.

A succession of poor crops and the economic consequences of the 1848 revolution threatened the livelihood of the people of Villaines who found themselves having to sell their baskets for a pittance. However, they were lucky in their village priest (by custom an influential character in the Touraine as elsewhere in France: for instance, another resourceful local cleric persuaded his parishioners not to destroy the castle-bridge at Chenonceaux during the 1789 revolution), the Abbé Chicoine who raised the necessary finance and persuaded basket-weavers not to compete fruitlessly against their neighbours and fellow workers. Thanks to these efforts, the Villaines men organized themselves into what eventually became the Coopérative de Vannerie.

Like basket-makers in other parts of France where willows grew easily, the

*Below* The tools of the basket-maker's trade. Shears, picking knives and bodkins all have to be razor-sharp to prevent slipping.

*Left and below* A weaver at work. She is sitting on a low bench and the piece she is making is pegged to a sloping board in front of her. The basket on which she is working is an oval *corbeille* of the kind that is often used to display seafood. Always working from left to right, she first makes the base, then she positions the upright stakes that will support the sides.

*Left* Basketry is strenuous uncomfortable work and each craftsman has to find the position that suits him best, always close to the floor. The canes are left uncut until the very end.

*Opposite* A variety of delicate weaves which shows off the basket-maker's skills.

*Below* Detail from a traditional tall bread basket used for storing baguettes.

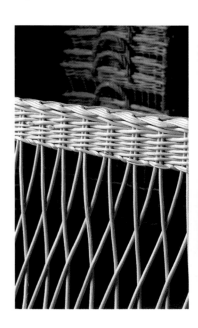

Villaines weavers produced articles that were used every day and in every way: all manners of baskets, for carrying, for sifting and sowing, for storing and displaying. Grapes, grains, bread, fruit, vegetables, bottles, crockery, traditional head-dresses and bonnets … everything had its special basket or pannier – flat, upright, round, tall, large or small, fine or thick. Poultry was taken to market in wicker cages, pet birds sang in osier cages, fish were caught in pots made of thin willow rods, babies slept in wicker cradles and people were even buried in willow coffins.

After the Second World War, wicker was soon replaced as the basic material for containers of everyday goods by plastic, lightweight metals and pressed cardboard. Disposability became the main criterion for such objects and Villaines had to diversify into making overtly decorative articles in order to survive. The late Fifties and Sixties were the era of wicker mirror frames, needlework baskets, magazine racks and vase-holders. Heavier furniture, often combining wrought-iron and wicker, also flourished in the pages of magazines and in homes *à la mode*: wicker chairs and armchairs, tables,

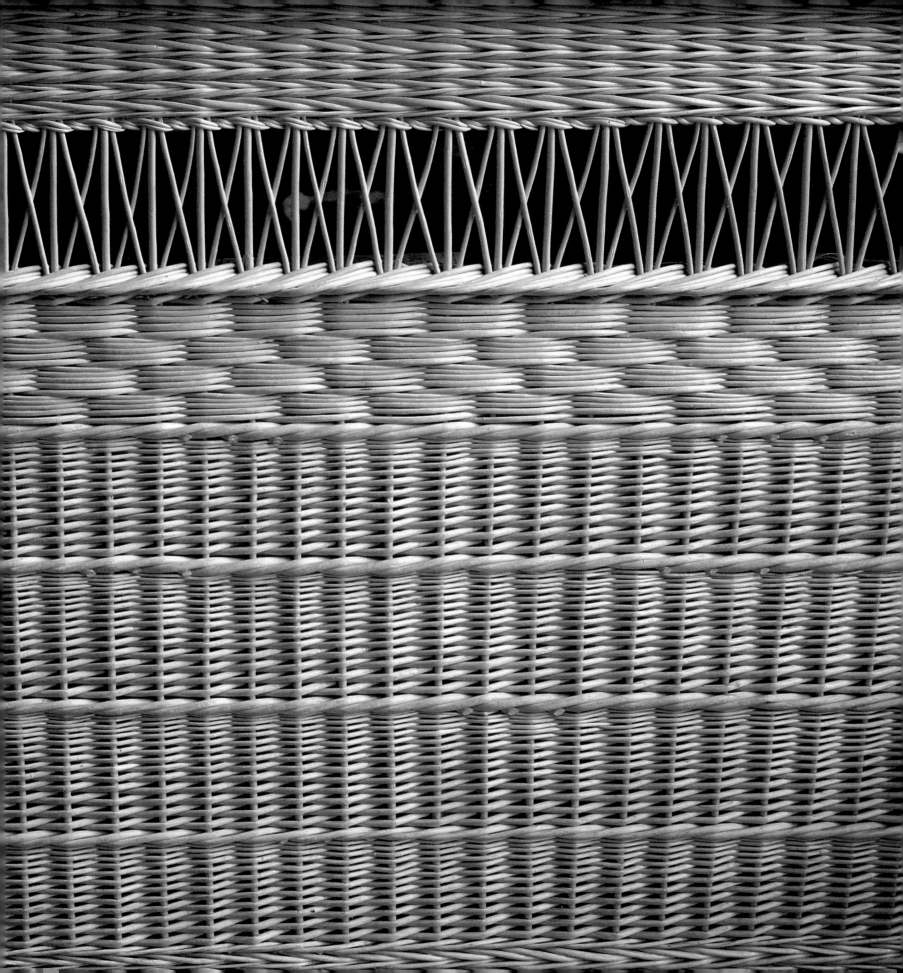

headboards, clothes racks and sofas were ubiquitous for a brief period.

*Plus ça change...* In the last decade of the century – very probably as a result of the growing interest in matters environmental – wicker containers are very much back in fashion. As in the old days, they are once more used for commercial purposes. Young delivery boys and girls can be seen again in the streets of Paris, Bordeaux or Toulouse carrying tall bread baskets – although perhaps not on the front of a heavy bicycle. The most famous baker in France, Lionel Poilâne, orders his bread-proving baskets and display cases at Villaines. Monsieur Poilâne is a passionate and articulate supporter of traditional crafts. A gifted 'communicator' with a big following through the media, his example has been followed by many suppliers besides the numerous outlets who sell his breads.

Much of Villaines' output is now sold to trade customers. Seafood restaurants display shellfish in open wicker baskets, other bakers are following in Poilâne's footsteps, and supermarkets use friendly osier containers to give their goods that down-to-earth genuine feel that appeals to modern consumers.

That the Villaines wicker is genuine and traditionally made is evident from the moment you enter the village. There are willows everywhere, most of them in small rows or beds, with a short thick trunk sprouting thin stalks which grow fast and tall and are cut and bundled every January when the sap is down. Only first-year growths tend to be used. They are sorted into bolts of different lengths and left to stand outside in pits of water until the late spring, by which time they are in full leaf. They are then stripped, and the delicate ivory-coloured rods are dried, bundled and stored in dark lofts or airy sheds until they are used.

Whereas traditional baskets are still made very much in the old way, in Villaines the ancient system has changed more than a little. The people you are likely to see flexing and coiling the sticks of willow when you visit the workshops will not be local boys and girls. It is also unlikely that these craftspeople were taught their skills by their fathers and grandfathers. The chances are they will be 'outsiders', trained at the National Basketry School at Fayl-Billot in the Haute Marne and employed as basket-makers by the Cooperative. After the basic two or three years' training, it takes another few years to become a competent professional and Villaines is one of the very few places in France where a newly qualified basket-maker can find a first job.

The Cooperative has kept its agricultural status and, in order to be a fully-fledged member, people have to own, grow and manage their own wicker production – making it practically impossible for newcomers to join. The Cooperative gathers the wicker of its seventy-plus members and acts as a marketing organization, distributing the wicker to the basket-makers, and centralizing orders, sales and dispatches.

The collective workshops are large rooms with high ceilings and plenty of

*Left* Straight from an old-fashioned nursery, a plain wicker cradle. The shop at Villaines-les-Rochers displays examples of what fine wicker furniture can look like.

*Below* Round osier basket.

An old picture of a man with a *van* is used by the Villaines Cooperative as a poster. A stylised version of the same image has become their logo.

light, all equipped with what looks like a large, long bath or trough where the willow is soaked for a couple of hours to make it more pliable and easier to use. The sticks are covered in cloth and kept as damp as possible.

The basket-makers work close to the ground, sitting on low benches, with a few tools at hand. Shears, pliers, knives, beaters and cleavers – and of course strong fingers – are all they seem to need to weave and shape the not-so-flexible rods. People work at very different speeds but – even if you spend only five or ten minutes watching – you can see the article emerging: a medium-sized flat basket takes a skilled worker about half an hour to make.

No wonder then that – after watching work that is so thoroughly done by hand – visitors are happy to spend money in the Villaines store, close by the workshops. The store and showroom is a large hall piled high with attractive merchandise, all bearing the Villaines logo of a basket-worker with a bundle of willow sticks. On the walls are several fine samples of old wicker-work – including a memorable ancient *van*, a large grain-sifting basket, and a funnel-shaped basket of the kind that was still used until a few decades ago by pickers during the *vendanges*. They would strap such a basket to their back and use it to carry sixty or so kilos (11 stones) of grapes to the cart.

The venerable baskets all look pretty good after centuries. This is nothing unusual, I was told. Wicker ages well and should keep for years. Occasionally it likes to be washed and scrubbed with soap and water, but there is no need to polish it and varnish would stop it from breathing.

The Villaines baskets are traditionally the colour of pale almonds but buff wicker has been so popular with visitors, particularly from Britain, that their tastes have been accommodated. Whether you want ivory, buff or dyed wicker, a cheese board, a child's armchair, a solid basket for carrying logs or shopping, an elegant open flat basket for cut flowers or a pretty little bread basket, you will find it hard to leave the Cooperative empty-handed.

## TO REPAIR OR NOT TO REPAIR:
## A CRAFTSMAN'S DILEMMA

When Claude le Corre's father taught him how to make potato baskets as a boy, Monsieur le Corre Père's friends all made fun of him. Your son will never earn a living making baskets, they said. You are wasting your time… Decades later Claude le Corre has to admit that the gloom merchants were partly right. Of the eighty basket-makers living and working in the village of Saint Méloir des Ondes – just outside Cancale near Saint-Malo in northern Brittany – before the war, he is the only one still involved in the business. He has also had to diversify to survive and he stopped making potato baskets a long time ago.

Potato baskets had been his father's speciality. Year in year out, in the few

*Left and opposite* Claude le Corre has kept a work area at the back of his shop. It gets plenty of light from the window looking out on the garden and is mostly used for repairs. Here Monsieur le Corre is re-caning a headboard. Repairs are time-consuming and not really worthwhile financially but they bring potential new customers into the shop.

weeks before the beginning of the harvest, le Corre regularly sold the 2,500 large oval baskets he had spent the rest of the year making with his fellow basket-workers (he employed several people). Each basket was used as a way of measuring the 50 kilos (1 hundredweight) of locally grown potatoes it could hold. Many of these spuds made their way across the sea to Britain where the baskets were destroyed – a wasteful practice perhaps, but certainly a source of more work for the basket-makers of the region.

The war put an end to the trade and, in the post-war years, new regulations and the advent of cheaper materials meant that demand never picked up again. The old potato baskets had become obsolete. Fortunately, Claude le

Corre had taught himself how to work with cane to make seating and other kinds of basketry. He was kept busy throughout the Fifties and Sixties making cane furniture and ornaments as well as vegetable and seafood baskets.

However, it takes six hours to cane a chair, three hours to finish a good-sized basket and he now finds it impossible to make a profit out of his hand-crafted articles. By the time he has added the cost of buying in the materials – cane is imported from Asia and, unlike the basket-weavers of Villaines, he does not cultivate his own willows – and the cost of his own time, there is no way Monsieur le Corre can sell goods at a competitive price.

For this reason his shop is full of articles he has bought in from outside – often imported from abroad. As he has a good eye and knows what he is doing, they are well chosen. Also, as he is not greedy – he reckons he should have charged more realistic prices when the going was good – the merchandise on display is not over-priced. There are bundles and stacks of cane strips and willow sticks in a corner of the shop, next to a child's armchair Monsieur le Corre made for his now grown-up son and kept as a souvenir.

If somebody brings in a basket that needs a new handle or a chair or headboard that needs repairing, le Corre finds it hard to turn down the request. He looks at the article severely – the chances are it will be mass-produced and come from one of the sprawling monster hypermarkets that have sprung up in the outskirts of Saint-Malo or Rennes, as they seem to be doing outside every large city in France – but he will repair it for old time's sake and to keep his hand in. The customer will walk out with a better article than they brought in. The story has a happy ending as, more often than not, the customer will also buy something new in Monsieur le Corre's shop.

A sturdy potato basket.

*Above* Monsieur Hérisset with one of his besoms.

## THE BESOM-MAKER

We are in the heart of the country, the flat lands of southern Brittany going towards the Anjou borders. In the low-ceilinged workshop, bundles of russet birch wood branches are piled up against a wall. Through the small windows, the sky looks drizzly grey. It is the tail-end of winter and the quiet is melancholy. Not so Monsieur Hérisset, besom-maker to the town of Rennes who cheerfully explains that he gets a great deal of satisfaction from 'winning

The making of a besom. First Monsieur Hérisset trims the birch twigs. Next he takes a bundle of them and roughly lines them up. He presses them down and ties them together with wire. Then comes more trimming and the besom is ready.

people back from plastic brooms'. For those of you who may not be familiar with the word 'besom', let me quickly quote the dictionary: a besom is 'a broom made with twigs'. *Voilà*!

Using a pair of strong secateurs, Monsieur Hérisset trims the besom he has just put together with the help of a few twists of wire and a simple-looking pressing machine. He then clips off unruly tendrils that stick out here and there and the finished besom is added to a stack. On a good day, perhaps with a little help from one of his sons, he will make between forty and fifty broom heads – no broom handles as these last much longer than the twigs and people use them time and time again until they become shrunken and shiny with age.

Old-fashioned though the job may sound, making besoms – for Monsieur Hérisset at least – is a steadier source of income than the making of baskets which he is also equipped to do. The latter are more time-consuming and the demand for them has been badly hit by competition from the Far East.

For the brooms there are very serious regular customers: the municipality of Rennes, Monsieur Hérisset's major customer, orders 3,000-4,000 brooms a year to keep the streets of the city clean. He also regularly supplies local villages. Unlike baskets, which can be repaired, besoms actually wear out quite quickly and need to be replaced.

The Hérissets have been besom- and basket-makers for several generations and Monsieur Hérisset learned his craft from his father and grandfather. The bundles of birch from neighbouring woodlands are cut in the mid-winter. When nothing suitable is available locally, Monsieur Hérisset drives his lorry 100 kilometres (60 miles) to get the right bundles. He relies on his eyes to

Unlike the birch twigs which do the actual sweeping work, the heavy handles last indefinitely. Monsieur Hérisset normally supplies besoms without handles.

gauge bundles, rather than on scales or measuring tape. A good bundle will be enough to make two or three besoms.

Birch wood keeps supple for a long time (up to eighteen months) and besom-making goes on throughout the year to meet orders. However, draughts and a fierce sun can toughen the wood and make it brittle. To make them more pliable for working, the twigs are given a good soaking before they are made into besoms.

Monsieur Hérisset fits a handle into the centre of a broom and the finished product looks very appealing. I test it on the earthen soil of the workshop. It is very heavy, but it handles well… a heap of dead leaves, small stones and bits of wire soon builds up. I am enjoying myself nurturing visions of energetic sweeping of steps and patio tiles on a fine summer's morning.

A small boy comes into the workshop. A future besom-maker? Probably not, as he seems much more interested in his toy tractor than in his grandfather's work. Monsieur Hérisset reflects on being that age and remembers walking several kilometres to the weekly market at La Guerche with his grandpa to sell brooms and baskets.

The market still takes place every Tuesday, drawing over two thousand visitors to the old town with its pretty square and narrow streets dotted with half-timbered houses. However, Monsieur Hérisset's grandchildren won't remember trudging there on foot.

The finished article.

# WOODWORK AND FURNITURE

From the colourful painted dressers and chairs of the Alsace to the wedding *armoires* of Normandy and the cupboard beds of Brittany, the regional furniture of France is still made in the old ways. The artisans of wood are fewer than they used to be, but wherever you find yourself in France, someone, somewhere will tell you about Monsieur X who makes wonderful chests-of-drawers or Monsieur Z who is so good with marquetry and restoration. Signs advertising an *ébéniste* (cabinet-maker) or a *menuisier* (carpenter) are dotted along French country roads next to all those other familiar signs pointing the way to a *dégustation* or *produits régionaux* at such and such a *domaine*.

'Up-market' artisans still have a niche in the modern world. Further down the scale, their colleagues who once made the traditional simple wooden objects of everyday life – like clogs, boxes, spoons and coffee-grinders – have, alas, not been so lucky and the few survivors are hard to find. If, however, your heart is set on a piece of fine furniture, a hand-crafted musical instrument or even the pipe of your dreams, you will find it – at a price, perhaps, but you will not be disappointed.

Moreover, should you want a much-loved chair or table to be restored to its former glory, there will be someone to repair it. Those specialist artisans whose businesses have survived the blight of modern industry and mass-production do pride themselves on their work and are genuinely committed to their craft.

## A CABINET-MAKER IN NORMANDY

Once a Norman always a Norman. The twelve or so customers who every year invest in one of cabinet-maker Yves Tétrel's major pieces of traditional furniture, *meubles normands*, tend to come from Normandy. This is no coincidence. Whether they live in the old province or have 'emigrated' to Paris, Lyons or – more drastically still – Marseilles, the natives of Normandy

A woodcarver's tools. Assorted chisels and knives are carefully lined up on the workbench.

and even the descendants of natives of Normandy remain deeply attached to the style of furniture they were brought up with: the solidly handsome dressers, cupboards and clocks they remember seeing in their grandparents' *salon*, kitchen or dining-room.

Yves Tétrel lives and works in Normandy, close to Villedieu-les-Poêles where you can visit a splendid museum housing a substantial collection of traditional Normandy furniture. Compared to many of the artisans to whom I spoke while researching this book, Monsieur Tétrel's lot seems a particularly enviable one: not only is he very much his own boss, he also happens to be in the extremely fortunate position of being able to make a living out of selling a mere twelve 'commissioned articles' each year.

Yves Tétrel works entirely by himself. After a period of hiring help and taking on young apprentices, he decided that the complicated administrative procedures and paperwork involved in employing staff simply created too much extra work. The increased production was just not worth the added bureaucratic problems. He knows what he is talking about because he was in charge of a twenty-five-strong workshop making plywood furniture before he went solo to start his own business. He does really prefer to work on his own at his own pace, without interruptions.

His workshop came as a bit of a surprise. After visiting many an untidy cramped *atelier* where artisans seemed to have to wade through piles of odd bits and pieces to find a particular tool or item, Monsieur Tétrel's large, light and airy workspace was memorably spacious and uncluttered. On starting work as a cabinet-maker, he planned the workshop and built it by himself, across the garden from the house where he lives with his wife and two children. When I was there last, panels for the bodies of tall narrow clocks with nipped-in middles, known as *horloges demoiselle* (maiden clocks), were awaiting further work.

Ever since he was nine or ten years old, Yves Tétrel knew he wanted to work with wood, with his own tools. His own father worked in agriculture, but Yves was a determined young man and ended up doing what he most wanted. However, he feels strongly that not enough is done to inspire young children and encourage them to take up crafts at an early age.

Of the various stages in the cabinet-making process, the one he enjoys most is that of sculpting the wood. Tétrel spends many happy hours at his workbench meticulously carving the traditional motifs that have always adorned Normandy furniture: flowers, fruit and leaves, doves' nests, medallions, garlands and baskets. All these motifs are symbols of happiness, love and prosperity. The traditional Normandy wedding gift to a young couple was a large cupboard in which they stored their most precious belongings throughout the rest of their lives. The gift was solemnly presented to the pair by the bride's parents and this custom of giving a cupboard rather than money survived until very recently.

*Left* Carving a decoration on a housing for a traditional Normandy clock.

Linen, best clothes, mementoes, papers, relics… all were kept in the treasured hefty oak *armoire*. The doves, flowers and fruit carved on the cupboard lightened and personalized what could be an overwhelming piece of furniture. After this essential cupboard, over the years – if the family finances allowed – couples gradually bought other pieces of furniture, such as a dresser or a clock. The cupboard, however, always came first.

Charity begins at home: in his first year as a self-employed cabinet-maker, the first pieces of furniture that Yves Tétrel made were a cupboard and a dresser which he kept for himself. Together with a Tétrel clock, they have pride of place in the impeccable family sitting-room. Even now, after several years in business, he has genuinely to 'like' a piece of furniture and to feel totally satisfied with it before he shows it to a client.

People come to him because they have seen his work: possibly in a trade fair, sometimes at the home of a friend or relative. He has a lot of 'repeat' customers – many of them people who are in their forties and feel that the

time has come to treat themselves to something nice to replace the simple furniture they have been using so far.

In the showroom next door to the workshop, several pieces of furniture are displayed: traditional cupboards with two doors, different kinds of dressers, cabinets, chests of drawers and clocks (the works are made elsewhere). Most are impressive and on the large side, Louis-Quinze in spirit, with straight or triangular cornices, and decorated with delightful carved motifs.

Yves Tétrel went to a great deal of trouble researching traditional Normandy motifs, copying specific details from old originals until his

*Opposite and right* A gleaming vintage Tétrel clock and dresser take pride of place in the family's living-room.

technique allowed him to work creatively and still keep the spirit of the ornament. All the furniture that comes out of his workshop is signed and dated, and no two pieces are completely identical.

He uses various woods, including oak, chestnut, some pine and mahogany, and gleaming copper or steel trimmings. None of this is varnished: instead, the finished furniture is given a thorough polishing before it leaves the workshop. However, Tétrel reckons it takes at least a year for a cupboard or a dresser to mature to its characteristic timeless deep sheen. He says he can tell a lot about his customers from the state of their ('his') furniture if he visits them a few years after they have purchased something: some clearly anxious people over-polish and scrub too hard, while others are neglectful – perhaps a sign of unhappiness or depression… 'No more psychology: what good furniture needs is just *un peu de jus de coude et un morceau de chiffon* (a little elbow grease and a piece of rag).

## MAKING BRETON BAGPIPES

Facing resolutely away from France, Brittany is an independent-minded province where deeply rooted local traditions are alive and thriving. One of the strongest of the Breton traditions is music-making, involving several thousands of people who play or give performances on a regular weekly basis throughout the province.

This they do neither in a self-conscious effort to keep their identity alive

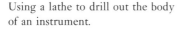

Using a lathe to drill out the body of an instrument.

nor in an attempt to amuse tourists and visitors – although folk music and dancing are great entertainment. For many Bretons their musical culture is a living thing. A *bagad* is the name they give to a group of musicians playing the *binou*, the bagpipe of Brittany, and the *bombarde*, a robust country cousin of the oboe. (The teaching of the Breton language in schools may have been forbidden for a hundred years but many words remain in use to this day.)

Like several other contemporary Breton instrument-makers, Gilbert Hervieux and Olivier Glet came to choose and learn their craft as a result of their music-making and love of the sharp tones of the traditional tunes. This is different from the more usual pattern of wind instrument-makers being born in families of instrument-makers. Right at the other side of the country, in the Lorraine at Mirecourt, the traditional capital of French stringed instrument manufacture, master violin-makers tend to pass on technical expertise and trade secrets from father to son.

Both self-taught and both from the same region, Messrs. Hervieux and Glet met while they were doing their military service and thus had plenty of

*Top left* A craftsman's eye. Olivier Glet checks the body of a *bombarde*. The *bombarde* of Brittany (*right*) is related to the oboe but sturdier-looking. To satisfy their knowledgeable and demanding clientèle of Breton music fanatics, Hervieux and Glet make 40 different models of *bombarde* available in 9 different tonalities.

opportunities to discuss and practise their common hobby. They borrowed money from their families and went into partnership to make *bombardes*, Breton bagpipes and transverse flutes. Many early days were spent producing lamp stands as a good way of improving their wood turning skills.

They make about 500 musical instruments each year, one-third of them *bombardes*. The market is limited but enthusiastic and most of their production is sold in Brittany, but the rest goes to places where Bretons have settled along the Loire – particularly near Angers – and in Paris. Apart from the Breton demand, Messrs. Hervieux and Glet have loyal foreign customers in Germany, Britain, the USA and Canada – countries where there is a genuine and widespread interest in folk music.

Business is good and instrument-making keeps them too busy to have time to play themselves as much as they would like, but they practise regularly. Sometimes they also go on tours with other musicians. A recent and much-enjoyed tour of Louisiana with two different bagpipes, an accordion and a *bombarde* had been very complicated to organize but a commercial success for their instrument business.

One of the aspects of their work Hervieux and Glet are particularly enthusiastic about is creating spare parts or modifying parts of the instrument in order to help musicians change the tonality of their *bombarde* or *biniou*. This would enable them to play other kinds of music, moving from the diatonic to the chromatic. Breton music, ever-evolving, ever-popular, would become still more varied and flexible – an exciting development which Hervieux and Glet feel is likely to happen in the not-too-distant future.

## THE LAST OF THE CLOG-MAKERS

When I first started to think about the country crafts of France, clog-making came high on my list. Perhaps this was because of the stories I had read as a child, many of them featuring *un sabotier*, a clog-maker, who was also a bit of a part-time magician. Sometimes wicked, but usually kind to the heroes of the adventure, he invariably lived deep in the heart of a thick dark forest full of dangers. I also remember seeing clogs on market stalls, in the village cobbler's shop and, of course, on people's feet.

Not on mine, though. I did try a pair once, but they felt most uncomfortable. Keep trying, said the cobbler, you'll get used to it. However, my mother thought that sandals were better for little girls' feet anyway, so the only pair of clogs I got to wear was years later when I bought a very unauthentic little black pvc pair in London about 1978.

In the end, finding a genuine practising country *sabotier* was not an easy job: there are only a handful of clog-makers left in France, scattered in very remote areas. Still I was determined. So we found ourselves on a suitably wet

Stacked up to the rafters with piles of wood and boxes, Monsieur Harlais's workshop has a certain labyrinthine quality.

First cleave and quarter your length of wood ... Monsieur Harlais makes a clog. He is using tools that have been in the family since his grandfather's days.

and windy night in March, knocking at the door of a large shed of an *atelier* somewhere in the depths of the Breton countryside.

If Monsieur Harlais' workshop was not the forest hut of my childhood books, it too in its way was unforgettable. It took us a while to see the owner: higgledy-piggledy piles of wood planks, trunks, half-made clogs, embryonic toys and utensils were stacked up to the rafters. Where there was no wood, there were antique machines and tools, boxes, ropes and even a punch bag. Only a narrow path had been left clear, meandering from the door to Monsieur Harlais' workbench.

His greeting was very friendly. His two passions in life, he soon explained, are his work and children. He cannot resist playing with wood and constantly

starts making things which he never has the time to finish, not just now anyway – but he would, one day, even if it means continuing work until he is a hundred. The punch bag is for his son, when he is home from college and chatting to his dad in the workshop. Monsieur Harlais loves being visited by family and friends while he is working. I was quite reassured: clearly we had come to the good kind of *sabotier*, not the wicked species.

Monsieur Harlais learnt his craft from his grandfather. His own father died when he was 27, too young to pass on his expertise to young Marcel. When he started, there were several *sabotiers* in the area: local people wore clogs everyday. The average villager needed two or three pairs a year – some, such as blacksmiths and quarry workers, easily wore out seven pairs. Clog-makers

*Left* One almost ready hand-made clog …

… And now there are two (*above*). Monsieur Harlais readily admits that even a dedicated old-style craftsman such as himself tends to use a machine to bore and shape his clogs. It saves a lot of time and the result is still finished by hand.

worked all year round, demand dwindling in the spring when people started using up old split clogs or going barefoot.

Even the most ardent clog-wearer these days only needs to buy a new pair every two or three years. Marcel Harlais has seen all his colleagues go out of business. For him it still comes as a bit of a shock to remember that he is the only clog-maker left, not just in the area or even in the *département*, but probably for several *départements*.

He usually makes his clogs out of birch wood, a little dry but not too dry, cut into lengths. Woodpeckers and frosts are perennial enemies, both causing the wood to split. He uses machines – the ancient equipment I had first noticed lining the path through the brimming workshop – but still sometimes makes clogs by hand, using the tools his grandfather made.

Monsieur Harlais shows us how. First, he roughly shapes the outside of the clog, then he bores the inside with various tools, including a gimlet shaped like a spoon and one for the heel that looks just like the world's toughest shoe-horn.

Bespoke clogs? Well, feet do come in very odd shapes. The strangest pair of clogs he ever made was to fit someone with a huge bunion on his toe… A prudent person with bizarre feet also once commissioned twenty pairs 'to see him through'.

The 'standard' clogs Monsieur Harlais sells in his shop look very appealing, rows and rows of them ready to accommodate whole families of feet, from the gigantic to the tiny. Some are light plain polished birch, some are darker and decorated, others are leather-trimmed, and there are some with a jaunty

Leather-trimmed clogs.

turned-up toe which could well be dancing clogs. I notice that, mindful of today's more tender feet, Monsieur Harlais provides slippers to line his clogs – it certainly wasn't like that in my village!

I explore the shop with the help of Madame Harlais. Since it is so hard to make a living from clogs alone, Marcel Harlais makes other wood articles and Madame Harlais buys in additional merchandise for the shop which she manages. I notice handsome salad bowls, a whole array of large flattish spoons – for pancakes, I am told – and what look like old-fashioned washerwomen's laundry beaters. Irresistible! I buy several spoons (after all, I do make pancakes about once a year and I have friends who are into making jam and marmalade), a beater (to use as a cheese-board) and a very attractive mortar with a large rim and a pestle that I have just learned is a traditional nutcracker. I get great use from them all and have just heard that one particularly large spoon is a great deterrent when brandished occasionally at energetic three-year-old twins.

## WOOD TURNING:
## BOBBINS AND BALUSTRADES

In the world of crafts, one thing leads to another and one artisan often introduces you to a colleague. When I visited the lace-makers of Bayeux (see page 118) I became curious about the delicate little wood bobbins they were using. The bobbins – which are known as *bloquets* in the region – were all elaborately decorated, suitable instruments for the exquisite lace patterns that were emerging from them. Some bobbins had complicated chequered patterns; others a loose ring attached to them: they all seemed to be the result of a great deal of individual attention.

'You must go and see Bernard, Mylène Salvador's colleague,' Fabienne Ros told me. 'He knows all there is to know about bobbins.' Bernard's surname, I soon discovered, was Salvador. Any relation? Well, yes, he is Mylène's husband. I found Monsieur Salvador smoking a pipe and pondering figures on a computer print-out in the office over his workshop on Place des Pommes. It was only a short walk from the Conservatoire de la Dentelle (compact Bayeux has much to recommend itself as a location if you decide to go on a craft trail).

Bernard Salvador cuts a bit of a Renaissance figure. A former teacher of philosophy turned artisan, he belongs to the elite group of the *Meilleurs Ouvriers de France*, and has not abandoned hope of finishing his thesis on the philosophy of art. As a boy he had loved fiddling with wood, spending as much of his spare time as possible in a friendly local carpenter's shop where he 'toyed' with a lathe. It was love at first sight and, as his craftsmanship increased, he was soon able to turn his hobby into a lucrative pastime.

He perfected his professional training in the Jura, the thickly forested

Bernard Salvador turns a segment of ordinary ox bone into a uniquely exquisite bobbin. As a finale to his demonstration, he has lifted a loose ring from the mass of the bobbin (*bottom right* on the photograph). This little circle traditionally symbolizes a lace-maker's wedding ring.

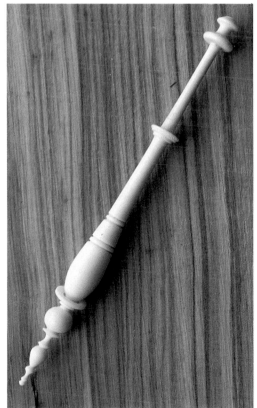

region traditionally home to many French masters of wood turning. The masterpiece he created for his *MOF* exam is still in the window of the *atelier*, a beautiful complex *torsade* creation of a spindle and wheel inlaid with precious woods. *Torsades*, or twisted cord effects, are his 'speciality', as is fine marquetry, and he is equally happy making balustrades, chess boards or tobacco pots.

Like the good teacher he clearly must have been before he abandoned the classroom for the workshop, Bernard Salvador made a bobbin in front of us to help me understand the process. The bone came from an ox, said Monsieur Salvador, flourishing a very authentic butcher's wrapping. He treated it with an aluminium silicate and sawed and polished it into a rough cylinder about 10 cm (4 in) long. Then, in the next few minutes, as he gradually turned the cylinder into a uniquely shaped bobbin, I learned that bone was the oldest precious material, found in the most ancient of tombs. Bobbins were once made of expensive woods, or sometimes of ivory which is much more fragile than bone. Every region had its traditional bobbins and there were dozens of different shapes and types.

By then Monsieur Salvador was lifting a ring out of the mass of the bobbin. He eased it off very gently, water dripping continuously over the bobbin to keep the temperature down. I found out the meaning of such loose rings on bobbins I had noticed earlier: when a lace-maker gets married, it is an old Normandy custom to lift a symbolic ring out of a precious bobbin.

Suddenly there it was, a perfect bobbin in gleaming white bone. All that was needed to finish it off was a touch of bleach and a little buffing, said Monsieur Salvador, eyeing the bobbin critically. He was quite pleased with his handiwork. Perhaps he would keep it as a prototype – bobbins are machine-made and very few hand-crafted, but the eye and the hands of a skilled artisan are still needed to make the models that will be used to guide the machines' work.

Less than fifteen minutes had passed since I had been shown the rough bone cylinder and the wrapping paper. I believe it took Bernard Salvador, in true artisan style, longer to locate his bleaching kit – a tub, a bottle of hydrogen peroxide and some ammonia – than it did to make the bobbin.

## THE BRETON BOAT-MAKER

Among corrugated iron sheds, shapeless pre-fabs and forlorn goods depots, Charles Fresneau's workshop stands out, a fine nave-like wood structure, in a sprawling suburb that is halfway between between a light industrial zone and a residential area.

Charles Fresneau is a maritime carpenter working near Saint-Lunaire, close to Dinard in Brittany. He built his workshop himself, not once but twice:

Inside the workshop an elegant rowing boat is being renovated.

having started it in 1986, he completed it just in time for the big storm of October 1987. Down came the workshop in the night, like much else in the region which was right in the path of the destructive gale.

A new workshop soon grew up. Made of plain pine, with large skylights and windows facing the south-west away from the heat of the strongest sun, it makes a harmonious setting for the boats on which Monsieur Fresneau is working and helps to temper the rigours of the climate. Three cats are on constant mouse patrol – one of them is quick to eat Monsieur Fresneau's mid-

*Left* The rowing boat being restored is made of light mahogany, a wood that was recently arrived from the New World and much in vogue when the *yole* was built in the middle of the last century.

*Above* Monsieur Fresneau carefully positions and fits in a polished rowing bench.

morning croissant the minute he leaves it behind to show me around. I am surprised at the wooden floor-boards: is it necessary in a workshop? Well it keeps the place warm in winter, and if you drop a chisel or some other fine tool, it won't get chipped.

Fresneau is building a large yacht for a private customer – an order that is

*Left* Once Charles Fresneau has finished with it, every handsome inch of the rowing boat will be as good as new. But the boat will be a museum piece and will never have to take to the water again.

*Above* A rowing bench has been smoothed back to a perfect finish. It is almost ready to be fitted back into the boat (see previous pages).

Wood everywhere you look. Charles Fresneau used pine to build the workshop he designed himself. The floor too is made of wood. Fresneau believes this is the best possible environment for the boats he makes and repairs.

For the past three years nearly half the workshop has been taken up by a yacht which Charles Fresneau is building for a client.

taking 6,000 hours and three years to finish. He could have done it faster but, then, the client could not have kept up with the regular payments! So Fresneau staggered the work, dividing his time between this project and restoring three boats for the Musée de la Marine, a prestigious commission which makes him very happy.

Of the three boats he is restoring, two are relatively uncomplicated: there is a *pointu* (the sturdy little fishing boat of the Mediterranean) that comes from Saint Tropez, and a sailing boat from Le Havre known as a *cormorant*. The real challenge is a *yole*, an elegant rowing boat built around 1850 seating 4 oarsmen.

This used to belong to the Martell cognac family and for eighty years or so regularly sailed on the Seine. During the Second World War it was hidden under a heap of straw. It survived unnoticed and was left to accumulate the dust and dirt of ages. So much so that when Monsieur Fresneau started cleaning it some time ago, it soon lost half its body weight. The boat is made of light mahogany from Martinique with a beautiful rose moiré effect. It practically had to be re-built, but restoration work is quite different from building work. A small detail like seaworthiness, for instance, does not come into it. The *yole* will never be set on water again, but it has to look as much as possible as it did in the old days, when it sped under the bridges of Paris in all its sleek glory.

Fresneau has old pictures and plenty of documentation to work from – an advantage of working with a museum. He did have to consult specialist restorers on some points of detail as the woods had to be exactly like the ones that were used a century and a half ago. Not an easy task – Fresneau admits that he was tempted to give up on several occasions. Now that what was once a wreck is looking like a beautiful museum-piece of a rowing boat, he is glad that he and the museum decided to gamble on the *yole* being 'restorable'.

How did the Musée de La Marine pick him for the job? It is a very small world, he explains. Literally, for not many people can afford the cost of hundreds of hours of top craftsmanship and materials. Everything works by word-of-mouth – his clients tend to talk to each other about yachts and boats. The museum came to hear of him and decided he was the right man for its restoration programme.

Even if many craftsmen were lost as a result of the plastic boat boom of the sixties, traditional yacht-making has remained very much the activity it was at its heyday between the wars. Fresneau came late to the trade – his parents were teachers – and learned the job working for local shipyards, starting with painting, stripping and stopping-up. He read a lot, learning English as he went along because most of the relevant publications came from the USA and Britain. Several old volumes of yachting books and magazines and the like are stacked here and there on shelves in the workshop, splattered with wood dust and shavings. Dealers of antiquarian books would give a lot for Charles Fresneau's reference materials.

## THE QUEST FOR THE PERFECT CHAIR

Having admired the caning of the backs of the rowing benches in Charles Fresneau's *yole*, we found ourselves later on in the day knocking at the door of the man responsible for this beautiful work.

For the first ten minutes I felt that our long detour (it was not an easy place to find) had been in vain. Alain Billon was very pleasant but rather unwilling to talk about his caning work. In his opinion, the cane and straw seating for which he had acquired a reputation over the past ten years was almost a thing of the past.

From making just the seating he has moved on to the whole chair. Re-caning and restoring led him to wonder why some chairs were so much better crafted than others and some worth repairing while others should simply be burnt. Alain came to the conclusion that chair-making had gradually lost much quality and *finesse* in the last century and a half. So he studied the techniques and materials of the eighteenth century, when chairs were at their finest, and started to make his own.

To increase his skills he is learning wood sculpting and painting at a local college. For him, the true artisan has to keep on developing. He shows us several examples of his work: there are some chairs in the spirit of Louis-Quinze and Louis-Seize furniture, and some in the Spanish style.

We enthuse that these are the best pieces of work we have seen in days and Alain becomes a little more talkative. He tells us about the problems of aging birch wood, about painting wood with rabbit's tails, about using a garden roller to get rid of knots in the straw before you start working with it.

He then takes us to the field where he grows his own rye, tiny sprouts still in the March afternoon before they shoot up to their final height of around 2 metres (6 ft). Unfortunately, they are too small to photograph.

As we leave, I make a note of the route to Alain's house and workshop. I shall save my pennies and come back next year. By the time this book is published, Alain Billon's work will be definitely worth a big detour.

Raw materials for Alain Billon's caning work (*left*). An artisan who believes in constantly experimenting, he has moved on from caning to trying to make the perfect chair.

Spring in the Provence maquis. In the hills behind Cogolin the briar trees are in blossom.

A briar root. Away from its natural environment it has a bizarre appearance. Yet the craftsman's hand will transform it into things of simple beauty.

## FIRST AGE YOUR BRIAR: THE PIPES OF COGOLIN

French pipe-makers – like French chefs – have long known that the only way to create a great product is to use the very best ingredients. That is why Cogolin in the Var is the heart of French pipe-making. It is recognized that the briar shrubbery of the surrounding countryside possesses all the qualities needed in a good pipe. Monsieur Charles Courrieu, the leading Cogolin pipe-maker, told me with quiet pride that many of the celebrated pipes of Saint-Claude in the Jura were, in fact, made with briar wood from the Cogolin *maquis*. In fact, the pipe blocks of many other renowned pipe-makers are made *chez Courrieu*.

The huge briar root is first dug up by hand on a wet wintry day, making sure that the wood is damp enough not to crack and that enough remains

Still life in Charles Courrieu's
workshop: a briar root, blocks and
half-finished bowls.

A collection of drill bits used for
drilling pipe bowls out of blocks of
briar root.

Monseiur Courrieu *fils* working a
lathe.

A heap of embryo pipe bowls.

From classic simple pipes to ornate creations there are hundreds of models from which to choose.

behind to preserve the growth for future years. (The idea of 'sustainable resources' is so ingrained in the philosophy of the French craftsman that it quite literally goes without saying, *ça va sans dire*. Something will be left for future generations of pipe-makers: Monsieur Courrieu's son has already started working with his father, who had himself followed in the footsteps of both his father and grandfather.)

Then the root-wood is cut into blocks, each the rough shape of a standard pipe. These pipe blocks are then boiled in plain water for several hours to get rid of any sap and resin, and left to dry for three to five years. This is so that the resulting material will produce a pipe that is light in the mouth and the hand, which will subtly take colour from the tobacco without blackening and above all, never ever over-heat or split. For a pipe-maker, a cracked pipe is the greatest shame.

Bad pipes can have a bitter taste. To be good, I was told, a pipe must be scrupulously neutral: it may soften and round-out the taste of the tobacco but it should never intrude with its own flavour notes. It is perhaps above all for this 'flavour neutrality' that the briar wood of Cogolin, when appropriately treated, is most highly prized.

When the pipe block is ready to be carved, it is secured in a vice if it is to be a unique hand-crafted model, or on the first of three lathes if it is part of a series. Then the turning begins. All the finished pipes are individually buffed and polished to a fine smoothness. Even to a non pipe-smoker, they feel good to handle. Their natural colour is a warm veined auburn, but there are, of course, many other finishes.

The Courrieu trademark is discreet in the extreme. You have to look closely at a pipe to see the words *vieille bruyère, Ch Courrieu, Cogolin* alongside the little cockerel that is the symbol of the town. But then, as they say, good wine needs no bush.

# Bibliography

*Baccarat* Jean-Louis Curtis, Thames and Hudson, 1992

*Un Calendrier Traditionnel* Michèle Richet, in *La France et les Français*, Encyclopedie de la Pléïade, 1972

*Guide du Chineur* Jean Bedel, Larousse, 1989

*Le Compagnonnage* Revue des Métiers d'Art no 35, 1988

*Coutellerie et Couteliers au XVIII siècle* Revue d'Auvergne no 503, 1986

*La Dentelle de Bayeux* Marie-Catherine Nobécourt et Janine Potin, Editions Bertout-Luneray, 1991

*La Dentelle Illustrée* Conservatoire de la Dentelle de Bayeux, 1989

*France in the 1980's* John Ardagh, Penguin, 1982

*Le Maréchal Forgeron de Village* Martine Jaoul, Editions de la Réunion des Musées Nationaux, no 119

*Métiers d'Art Français Contemporains* Revue des Métiers d'Art no 32, 1986

*Pays de Loire* Revue des Métiers d'Art no 21, 1982

*Le Guide Poilâne des Traditions vivantes et marchandes* Lionel Poilâne, Robert Laffont, 1989

*La Poterie de Noron au Service du Grès* Xavier de Lorraine, in Revue des industries d'Art, no 135, 1978

*La Poterie Commune à décor baroque* François Carrazé, Bulletin de l'association Polypus, 1987

*Poteries et Potiers, Cliousclat*, Drôme, 1983

*Potiers et Poteries du Pays de Dieulefit* Association Patrimoine Potier, Dieulefit, Drôme, 1986

*Verre Contemporain à Dieulefit, 20 ans d'échanges internationaux*, Plein-Cintre éditions, 1990

*Le Vitrail Français Moderne* Revue du Centre International du Vitrail, no 4, 1989

# Addresses Visited

La Verrerie de Biot
Chemin des Combes, 066410 Biot
93 65 03 00

La Poterie Provençale
06410 Biot
93 65 63 30

Verrerie Le Pontil
26220 Dieulefit
75 46 45 48

Nicolas and Olivier Sourdive
Cliousclat
26270 Loriol sur Drôme
75 63 05 69

Valdrôme
135 avenue de Romans, 26000 Valence
75 43 35 05

Terres Cuites J. Sismondini
Route de Sillans, La Cascade,
83690 Salernes
94 04 63 06

Carrelages Alain Vagh
Route d'Entrecasteaux, 83690 Salernes
94 70 61 85

Vannerie de Villaines-les-Rochers,
37190 Azay-le-Rideau
47 45 43 03

Baccarat
30 bis rue de Paradis, 775010 Paris
47 70 64 30
and
Baccarat
54120 Baccarat
83 75 19 01

58 avenue Georges Clémenceau,
83319 Cogolin
94 54 63 82
(and in Paris)
129 rue saint-Honoré, 75001 Paris
40 28 03 19

Atelier Lorin
46 rue de la Tannerie, 28000 Chartres
37 34 00 42

Société Nouvelle des Faienceries de
Gien, 45500 Gien
38 67 00 05
(in Paris)
Boutique de la Faiencerie de Gien
39 rue des Petits Champs, 75001 Paris
47 03 49 92

Bernard Lissague
Société Mayaud-Lissague
49650 Brain-sur-Allones
41 52 03 33339

Bruno Pottier
827 boulevard Delessert, 49400 Saumur
41 67 37 87

La Taillerie de Royat
Boulevard de la Taillerie, 63130 Royat
73 35 81 25

Maison de la Coutellerie, 58 rue de la
Coutellerie, 63300 Thiers
73 80 58 86

Gilbert Hervieux & Olivier Glet
Le Val, 56350 Rieux
99 91 90 68

Charles Fresneau
La Ville aux Coqs, 35800 Saint-Lunaire
99 88 06 06

Claude Le Corre
Rue de la Gare, 35350 Saint-Méloir des
Ondes
99 89 12 06

Roger Hérisset
Les Grands Ormeaux
Rannee, 35130 La Guerche de Bretagne
99 96 32 21

Marcel Harlais
La Motte
35460 Saint-Brice-en-Cogles
99 97 76 49

Conservatoire de la Dentelle de Bayeux
Hotel du Doyen, 14400 Bayeux
31 92 73 80

Ateliers de l'Horloge, 14400 Bayeux
31 92 70 76

Bernard Salvador
5 Place des Pommes, 14400 Bayeux
31 21 35 99

Michèle Cosnier
61700 Dompierre
31 30 44 40

Atelier du Cuivre,
50800 Villedieu-les-Poêles
33 51 31 85

Fonderie Cornille-Havard
13 rue du Pont-Chignon,
50800 Villedieu-les-Poêles
33 61 00 56

Monsieur et Madame Dubost
14000 Noron-la-Poterie
31 92 56 15

Yves Tétrel
La Dorée
La Lande d'Airou,
50800 Villedieu-les-Poêles
33 51 27 30

Alain Billon
35190 Québriac
99 68 00 42

La Grange
83 Salernes, 94 70 62 94

# Craft Courses in France

## ILE-DE-FRANCE

### CERAMICS

Keramos
24 rue Violet, 75015 Paris
45 79 68 47

### JEWELLERY-MAKING

Académie du 11ème
29–37 rue des Trois Bornes, 75011 Paris
43 38 73 00

B.J.O. Formation
7 rue Jules César, 75012 Paris
43 42 27 00

### LACE-MAKING

Amicale des dentellières et brodeuses de
l'Ile de France
56 rue du Talus, 92500 Rueil-Malmaison
47 51 86 39

L'atelier de la dentellière
7 rue de Patay, 75013 Paris
45 86 14 78

### METAL-WORKING

Centre des métiers d'art
10 rue de Mandres,
94520 Perigny-sur-Yerres
45 98 92 07

### NEEDLEWORK

Cours de broderie Malbranche
17 rue Drouot, 75009 Paris
47 70 03 77

Institut supérieur de broderie d'art
13 rue de la Grange Batelière,
75009 Paris
48 24 14 20

### WEAVING

Atelier Dosne
15 rue Dosne, 75116 Paris
43 53 13 73

Atelier Nicole Valsésia-Lair
95 Boulevard Brune, 75014 Paris
47 07 21 01

Les Ateliers de l'Association pour le
développement de l'animation culturelle
(A.D.A.C.)
Maison des Ateliers, Terrasse
Lautréamont, 75001 Paris
42 33 45 54
or
9 boulevard Edgar Quinet, 75014 Paris
43 21 63 88
or
19 rue Camille Flammarion, 75018 Paris
42 55 72 40

Greta des arts appliqués
9 rue Pierre Bourdan, 75012 Paris
43 46 71 99

Manufactures nationales de Tapis et de
Tapisserie
1 rue Berbier du Mets, 75013 Paris
43 37 12 60

Métiers d'Autrefois Aujourd'hui
45 rue Lhomond, 75005 Paris
43 36 53 65

## EAST

### CERAMICS

Atelier du Revermont
Le Perron, 39190 Beaufort du Jura
84 25 10 26

### GLASS-MAKING

C.E.R.F.A.V.
rue de la Liberté,
54112 Vannes-le-Chatel
83 25 47 38

### LACE-MAKING

Association Renouveau et Promotion de
la Dentelle
Avenue de Lattre de Tassigny,
88500 Mirecourt
29 37 06 61 or 29 37 07 44

Conservatoire de la dentelle de Luxeuil
BP 77, 70303 Luxeuil-les-Bains
84 40 39 83

### WEAVING

Ateliers Artistiques Artisanaux d'Alsace
15 rue du Chanoine Brun,
68100 Mulhouse
89 56 23 27

Ateliers Comtois d'Expression
Treige de la Cordière, 39100 Dole
84 82 20 09

### WICKERWORK

Ateliers Artistiques Artisanaux d'Alsace
15 rue du Chanoine Brun,
68100 Mulhouse
89 56 23 27

Ateliers Comtois d'Expression
Treige de la Cordière, 39100 Dole
84 82 20 09

### WOOD-WORKING

Regains sur monts et forêts
Montadroit, 39240 Arinthod
84 35 70 97

## CENTRAL

### CERAMICS

C.N.I.F.O.P.
Route de Saint-Sauveur,
58310 Saint-Amand-en-Puisaye
86 39 60 17

### LACE-MAKING

Centre d'Enseignement de la Dentelle
au Fuseau
2 rue Duguesclin, 43000 Le Puy
71 02 01 68

A l'économe
10 rue Paul Chenavard, 69001 Lyon
78 28 20 18

Hôtel de la dentelle
29 rue du 4 septembre, 43100 Brioude
71 50 27 00

### WOOD-WORKING

C.N.I.F.O.P.
Route de Saint Sauveur
58310 Saint-Armand-en-Puisaye
86 39 60 17

## NORTH

### CERAMICS

Les Ateliers du Soleil
68 rue Monsarrat, 59500 Douai
27 88 75 12

C.R.E.A.R.
Château de Montvillargenne,
60270 Gouvieux
44 58 21 24

## LACE-MAKING

L'atelier du Chèvrefeuille
11 allée Schubert, 91410 Dourdain
64 59 94 67

La dentelle aux fuseaux
18 rue du Murget, 60300 Senls
44 53 37 85

Au fil des doigts
68 rue Casimir Delavigne,
76600 Le Havre
35 41 21 51

Conservatoire de la dentelle de Bayeux
Hôtel du Doyen, 14400 Bayeux
31 92 73 80

## WEAVING

L'atelier des Ormeaux
rue du Valhermeil,
95430 Auvers-sur-Oise
30 36 75 11

Ateliers de l'horloge
2 rue de la Poissonnerie
14400 Bayeux
31 92 70 76

C.R.E.A.R.
Château de Montvillargenne,
60270 Gouvieux
44 58 21 24

École régionale des Beaux-Arts
Hôtel d'Ollone, 72 rue de Bressigny,
49000 Angers
41 87 54 41

Lycée de Sèvres
21 rue du Docteur Gabriel Ledermann,
92310 Sèvres
46 26 60 10

## WICKERWORK

C.R.E.A.R.
Château de Montvillargenne,
60270 Gouvieux
44 58 21 24

## WOOD-WORKING

C.R.E.A.R.
Château de Montvillargenne,
60270 Gouvieux
44 58 21 24

# WEST

## CERAMICS

A.D.L.A.A.
Le Haut Bourge de Crouttes,
61120 Vimoutiers
33 39 22 16

C.E.D.T.E.
11 rue du Cap Horn, 33700 Mérignac
56 34 33 40

Université de Bordeaux
Domaine Universitaire, Esplanade des
Antille, 33405 Talence Cedex
56 84 50 10

## LACE-MAKING

Association Aquitaine Dentelle et
Costume
61 rue Wustenberg, 33000 Bordeaux
56 81 26 67

La Maison du Filet
Le Close de l'Éperon, 61360 La Perrière
33 25 96 29

## LEATHERWORK

A.D.L.A.A.
Le Haut Bourge de Crouttes, 61120
Vimoutiers
33 39 22 16

## WEAVING

Annie Dubois
Le Monteil, 87200 Saint-Junien
55 02 00 36

Maison des Métiers d'Art
2 rue des Portes Chanac, 19000 Tulle

La Poterie de Saint-Porchaire
13 route de Chambroutet,
Saint-Porchaire, 79300 Bressuire
49 74 22 40

## WICKERWORK

La Poterie de Saint-Porchaire
13 route de Chambroutet,
Saint-Porchaire, 79300 Bressuire
49 74 22 40

# SOUTHWEST

## CERAMICS

Académie Internationale d'Été de
Wallonie
29 rue du Serpont, B-6800 Libramont
61 22 54 79

Agir Céramique
Ferme de Regagnas, 30770 Alzon
67 82 01 67

C.E.P.F.O.R.
BP 192, voie 2, Labège Innopole,
31676 Labège Cedex
61 39 19 00

École de Céramique de Provence
3 traverse du Moulin, 13400 Aubagne
42 84 20 79

École Municipale des Arts
Jardin Massey, Place Henri Borde,
65000 Tarbes
62 93 10 31

Poterie à la Ferme
Pougavin, 32190 Marambat
62 06 34 77

Teranga, 12560 Saint-Laurent-d'Olt
65 47 41 10

## LACE-MAKING

Les dentellières du Sud-Ouest
6 rue des Vases, 31000 Toulouse
61 62 57 42

## WEAVING

A.R.P. Château de Pruines
12320 Saint Cyprien
65 69 81 32

Atelier de Calvisson
Grande Rue, 30420 Calvisson
66 01 23 91

C.E.P.F.O.R.
BP 192, voie 2, Labège Innopole, 31676
Labège Cedex
61 39 19 00

Filature des Landes
12580 Villecomtal
65 44 61 13

## WICKERWORK

Atelier de la Vis
Taussac par Pezenes, 34600 Bedarieux
67 23 25 85

## WOOD-WORKING

A.R.P. Château de Pruines
12320 Saint Cyprien
65 69 81 32

Atelier du Chien Vert
La Peyrière, 81470 Lacroisille
63 75 03 58

Centre Artistique Roland Delsol
La Brunie, 12700 Capdenac
65 64 63 78

Jean Conil
12430 Le Truel
65 46 43 12

Interface
Les Faïsses, 30120 Rogues
67 81 52 76

# SOUTHEAST

## CERAMICS

Atelier Michel Cayla
84210 St Didier
90 66 11 60

Atelier 3
Le Collet de Recoux, 83570 Correns
94 59 51 57

## WEAVING

Atelier Sayanoff
La Trinité, 04210 Valensole
92 74 84 06

La ferme de Valignon
36140 Crevant
54 30 10 03

La Vicarie
Lincel, 04870 Saint-Michel
l'Observatoire
92 76 68 17

# Craft Makers in France
## A source list

Listed below is a selection of craft makers in a number of locations throughout France. The publishers have endeavoured to make sure that the information is current, but take no responsibility for the goods or services offered by these suppliers. Inclusion in or exclusion from this listing does not imply any sort of approval or otherwise by the publishers.

**ART METAL FOUNDERS**
ARAINSTYLE
10, rue Monseigneur-Lavarenne, 69005 Lyon
(78) 37 01 72
DEBUISSON
Route du Lac, 83570 Carces
DRIESEN, Etains
103, rue Chevaleret, 75013 Paris
584 09 28

**CANDLEMAKERS AND WAX CRAFTS**
ATELIER DE LA BOUVAGNE (Sibuet)
8, rue du Ban-Thévenin, 01800 Meximieux
(74) 61.07.31
ATELIER DU SOLEIL (Granger)
Route de Repenti, 83590 Gonfaron
(94) 78 31 96
CARON G.
Le Guichard, Réaumont, 38140 Rives
(76) 05 70 79
GIBASSIER
57, rue du Pontel, 78100 St-Germain-en-Laye
958 53 38
MAT Jacqueline
'Atelier terre d'ocre', Bonrepos-Riquet, 31590 Verfeil
(61) 84 60 02

**CLOCKS**
BRANCIARD François
11, rue Sainte-Helene, 69002 Lyon
(78) 38 06 14
ESQUIVE Jean, Maitre horloger
30 rue de Paradis, 75010 Paris
FINIASZ C. Maitre horloger, diplomé de l'E.N.H. de Cluses
10 rue Saint-Jacques, 38000 Grenoble
(76) 44 50 02
GENDROT Jean-Claude, Horloger
12, bd St-Germain, 75005 Paris
033 18 84
JOURNE Michel, Horloger
30, rue de Verneuil, 75007 Paris
261 24 62

**DECORATIVE PAINTING, GILDING, ENAMELLING**
ALEXANE
13, rue Fermat, 31000 Toulouse
(61) 53 48 57
AGERON Roseline
5, rue d'Irvoy, 38000 Grenoble
(76) 21 39 68
AMADUE Nelly
31, rue des Ursulines, 78100 Saint-Germain-en-Laye
963 25 50
ATELIER VIRGINIE
20, rue du Vieux-Versailles, 78000 Versailles
953 64 71
AUBERT Annick
135, rue du Ger-au-Bois, 78220 Viroflay
926 49 42
AUBRY Michel
10, rue Saint-Michel, 54000 Nancy
(83) 36 36 65
AU BURON CLARY
17, Grande-Rue, 78480 Verneuil-sur-Seine
965 86 50
BARTHOUX Dominique
Clos Génissieux, N° 65, 38330 Saint-Ismier
(76) 52 30 49

BEZOMBES Roger
3, quai Saint-Michel, 75005 Paris
033 95 73
BONY Paul et Adeline
12, rue Jean-Ferrandi, 75006 Paris
222 11 88
BRAND Gérard
5, rue de Mars, 67210 Obernai
(88) 95 58 16
BRUNEAU André
14, rue de la Cour-des-Aides, 33000 Bordeaux
BUFFILE Jean
5, rue Irma-Moreau, 13100 Aix-en-Provence, Atelier: 2 bis, traverse de l'Aigle-d'Or, 13100 Aix-en-Provence
CARDON Marie, TOURNIER Antoinette
'La Soie Disante', 36, rue de Verneuil, 75006 Paris
261 23 44
CATELAIN Anne
4, rue des Pépiniéres, 69480 Anse
(76) 67 03 38
Exposition 'Aux Curieux', 3, rue Juiverie, 69005 Lyon
CREAC'H Anne
15, rue de Val-Martin, 78860 St-Norm-la-Breteche
480 80 92
DECORY Nicole
17, bd de la Republique, 13100 Aix-en-Provence
(42) 27 68 98
DUFRANE Annie
Grand-rue, Cotignac, 83570 Carcès
(98) 69 61 44
DUMETZ Micheline
9, place des Echoppes, 78310 Maurepas
FONTAINE Nicole
19, rue de Saintonge, 75003 Paris
278 21 05
FONTANEL Liliane
188, avenue de la Republique, 78500 Satrouville
913 59 83

FRINGANT Yvette et Jean-Pierre
13, rue Pasteur, Allamps, 54112 Vannes-le-Chatel
(83) 25 42 46
FYOT Jean-François
'Les eaux vives', Bouxietes-aux-Dames, 54250 Champigneulles
(83) 25 83 34
GASSER Daniel
51, rue de la Carpe-Haute-Robertsau, 67000 Strasbourg
(88) 31 20 74
JUNUSZ J. Laqueur
54, rue Tramassac, 69005 Lyon
LE JUNTER Colette
37, boulevard Carnot, 59000 Lille
MALLET Louis-Robert
8, rue Jonas, 75013 Paris
589 92 84
PALOMARES M.
22, av. des Marronniers, 78150 Le Chesnay
954 31 67
PINHAS Agnès
16, rue St-Antoine, 75004 Paris
272 77 38
PLICQUE-GURLITT Danielle
312 hameau des Hermines, 78480 Verneuil-s/Stine
971 93 32
PLOET Yves-Marie
31, rue du Vieux-Versailles, 78000 Versailles
POURRUT Odette
14, av. du Marechal-Leclerc, 33630 Cazaux
SABATAY Dan
5, allee Claude-Debussy, 78110 Le Vesinet
966 39 62
SAUZE Max
'La Bergerie', Les Vences, 13122 Ventabren
(42) 24 61 91
SERGE et MAÏTA
Place de l'Eglise, 81170 Cordes
(63) 56 01 55

SIFFER Yves
Ecole primaire, Dieffenbach-au-Val,
67220 Ville
(88) 85 60 21
VALLOIS Claude
3, rue au Péterinck, rue de la Monnaie,
59000 Lille
VILLANUEVA Simone
4, rue des Bécasses, 67000 Strasbourg
(88) 39 56 42
WOHLFAHRT Frank
Route de Rentenbourg-Singrist,
67440 Marmoutier
(88) 70 63 89

## FURNITURE

ANDRES Pierre
La Couronnelle, 47000 Cahors
(65) 35 73 70
ANTIMO
10, rue de la Salle, 54000 Nancy
(83) 35 39 47
BARILONE Maurice
18, rue des Côtes-de-Vannes,
78700 Conflans-Ste-Honorine
972 79 14
BARRIER Marc
'Le Grand Chemin', Lentilly,
69210 L'Arbresle
(74) 01 72 14
BART
179, rue de faubourg Saint-Antoine,
75011 Paris
307 24 75
BAYET Gilles
'Le Bessey', 38630 Les Avenieres
(74) 88 60 72
BIEBER Roland
4, Abbaye Saint-Evre, 54200 Toul
(83) 43 13 51
BOUSQUET Paul et Fils
Prade Salars, 12290 Pont-de-Salars
BRANDT M.
Rue de la Republique, 67920 Hoerdt
(88) 51 32 67
CAMPIN Jean et Jacques
75, rue de la Benauge,
33000 Bordeaux-Bastide
CHIRAT Georges
102, rue Bossuet, 69006 Lyon
(78) 24 09 39
CLAPIER Georges
1, rue St-Eucher, 69004 Lyon
(78) 28 62 43
CLAUDE Alain
39, rue de la Gare, 54460 Liverdun
(83) 25 74 91
DAIDE René
15, bd Carnot, 31250 Revel
(61) 83 54 74

DECANIS Maurice
Rovon, 38470 Vinay
(76) 36 77 10
DESGANS André
72, rue de la Benauge, 33100 Bordeaux
(56) 21 23 60
DETHU M. Sabotier
Route de Mont-de-Marsan,
41120 Roquefort
D'INGEO Maurice
14, rue des Violettes, 38000 Grenoble
(76) 96 77 62
DISSIDI
14 bis, passage de la Bonne-Graine,
75011 Paris
700 47 95
DUPONT Frères
Rue de Pierge, 59740 Felleries
(20) 61 05 38
FLAMARY et Fils
14, rue de Corréze,
19100 Brive-la-Gaillarde
(55) 24 14 94
FLORENT Bernard
40, rue Etienne-Dolet,
59184 Sainghin-en-Weppes
(20) 58 47 80
Exp. Artisanat Copeaux, 90, rue des
Sarrazins, 59000 Lille
FORTIN Piette et LARGETEAU
Michel
8, rue Orbe, 33500 Libourne
(56) 51 02 68
GAIRE Gérard
24 bis, rue des Bingottes, 54120 Baccarat
(83) 72 16 41
GILLET
Rue de l'Eglise, 59740 Felleries
HAENTGES Frères
6, rue Titon, 75011 Paris
371 25 45
HERTRICH Michel
218, rue des Allies, 67860 Epfig
(88) 85 50 12
JOLY Jean
70, avenue de Paris, rue des Vieux-
Chenes, 1200 Rodez
(65) 68 12 39
JOUAN Jean-Paul
10, rue Perronet, 75007 Paris
548 64 20
JUNG Bernard
3, route de Strasbourg, 67470 Seltz
(88) 86 51 12
LATTES Jean
9, avenue de Saint-Ferréol, 31250 Revel
(61) 85 51 83
LEVEAUD et BERTRAMD L.-J.
89, rue de la Benauge, 33100 Bordeaux
(56) 86 12 95

MALLASSI Jacques
38131 Sainte-Antoine
MARCQ Jean-Pierre
40, rue Etienne-Dolet,
59184 Sainghin-en-Weppes
(20) 58 47 80
Exp. Artisanat Copeaux
92, rue des Sarrazins, 59000 Lille
MAURY Georges
Route de Toulouse, 31250 Revel
(61) 83 55 74
MAYET Julien
Av. Joliot-Curie, Crolles,
38190 Brignoud
(76) 08 02 83
MEYER François
25, rue Gambetta, Rosieres-aux-Salines,
54110 Dombasles
(83) 48 11 72
MICHELOTTI
65, rue Sainte, 13007 Marseille
(91) 33 20 09
MOCQUE Jean et Fils
95, fg St Antoine, 75011 Paris
343 12 13
MONROZIER Alain
La Valette, 38350 La Mure
(76) 94 91 11–15 à La Valette
MONS Emile
21, bd Gambetta, 31250 Revel
(61) 83 51 65
MONTAUT J.-M.-Henri
44, allée Branly, 31400 Toulouse
NIETO Justino
2, rue Edouard-de-Ponter,
33250 Pauillac

## JEWELLERY

ALEX 5, avenue Alphonse-Fochier,
69002 Lyon
(78) 37 26 36
BERGHOLZ Richard
14, rue Bouffard, 33000 Bordeaux
(56) 48 97 80
BOLTZ Morand
27, rue du Maroquin, 67000 Strasbourg
(88) 32 33 28
BONILLO Jean-Claude
44, rue de Montmorency, 75003 Paris
272 26 73
BOROVI Janos, Bijoutier
2, rue du Cherche-Midi, 75006 Paris
222 67 43
CAIRE Gilbert
9, rue Gigodet, 69004 Lyon
(78) 28 71 44
CAMBOIS Martine
14, rue du Général-Galieri,
78220 Viroflay
926 46 39

COSTANZA
2, rue des Moulins, 75001 Paris
073 84 10
ERIPRET Frédéric
31, rue Pasteur, 78190 Trappes
051 28 74
GIBOULET C.
8, av. Marc-Sangnier à Villeurbanne
(78) 84 87 66
GOUDJI
45, rue Lepic, 75018 Paris
076 89 93
HAZARD Jacques
Villey-le-Sec, 54840 Gondreville
(83) 43 60 68
HECHT A.
5, rue des Francs-Bourgeois,
67000 Strasbourg
(88) 32 06 41
HECKMANN Pierre
57, rue Bonaparte, 75006 Paris
033 71 09
KLEIN André
126, avenue de Strasbourg,
54000 Nancy
(83) 35 12 69
LAURENT DRAY Arlette
46–48, rue Romain-Rolland,
38400 Saint-Martin-d'Heres
(76) 25 01 28
LAZON Lucienne
'L'alouette', Rue de Racinay,
78120 Rambouillet
483 08 92
MATHIEU Max Bernard
18, rue Gustave-Simon, 54000 Nancy
(83) 36 17 65
MILLIAT Henry
12, rue Pierre-Curie, 54500 Vandœuvre
(83) 55 45 33
PASCAL Jacques
12, rue Bellecordiere, 69002 Lyon
PELLETIER Claude
Chemin du Baou, 06410 Biot
(93) 65 12 75
RADISSON J.-P. Bijoux anciens et
modernes
9, rue de l'Arbre-Sec, 69001 Lyon
(78) 28 42 33
SCHAD Roland, Joaillier, createur
32, rue des Gravilliers, 75003 Paris
278 07 17
SOUCHE Jean-Paul et Michel. Orfevres
157, rue du Temple, 75003 Paris
TAVERNIER Marcel, Horlogerie,
bijouterie, orfèvrerie
62, rue Royale, 78000 Versailles
950 13 92
TRAYNARD Sibylle, Bijoutier
Entraignes, 38740 Valbonnais

## MUSICAL INSTRUMENTS

ALLAIN Tanguy, Anches de biniou
7, residence du Chêne,
78160 Marly-le-Roi
958 29 18
AUDINOT Jacques
15, rue de Leningrad, 75008 Paris
387 57 80
BAUM Robert
21, rue Claire, 67300 Schiltigheim
(88) 33 38 88
BAZIN Charles
Route de Vroville, 88500 Mirecourt
(29) 37 03 65
BOYADJIAN Alec
13, rue Michel-Perret, 69006 Lyon
CHEVRIER Bernard
9, rue Pierre-Curie,
33340 Lesparre-Medoc
(56) 41 09 03
DOMENGIE
13, rue Montbauron, 78000 Versailles
950 19 14
EMMONS Douglas
St-Clément-sous-Valsonne, 69170 Tarare
FREGUIN Dominique
23, boulevard Wilson, 67000 Strasbourg
(88) 32 39 42
GEROME Frères
12, rue Le Breuil, 88500 Mirecourt
(29) 37 11 85
GUG Rémy
2, rue des Ecrivains, 6700 Strasbourg
(88) 35 50 40
LESUEUR Daniel
11 bis, rue Montgallet, 75012 Paris
343 09 86
LOTTE François
14, rue Le Breuil, 85000 Mirecourt
MERCIER-YTHIER Claude
20, rue de Verneuil, 75007 Paris
260 29 36
OLIVEAU Claude
7, rue Jobbé-Duval, 75015 Paris
828 45 51
PORTEUS Derek
5, villa Daviel, 75013 Paris
589 66 51
SCHMITT Jean-Frédéric
23, rue d'Algerie, 69001 Lyon
(78) 28 01 95
SCHMITT Lucien
18, rue de Beau-Soleil, 38240 Meylan
(76) 90 54 39
VIAN Alain
8, rue Grégoire-de-Tours, 75006 Paris
033 02 69

## POTTERY AND CERAMICS

AUBERT François

'La Maison Blanche', Yolet-le-Doux,
15130 Arpajon-sur-Cere
(70) 47 41 76
BATEL J. et F.
Atelier la Remise,
31540 St-Felix-de-Lauragais
(61) 83 01 61
BAJARD Dominique
'La Chassagne', Sainte-Paule,
69620 Le Boyis-d'Oingt
BARACHANT Elie
Carrelages, R.N. 7, 13760 St-Cannat
(42) 28 21 34
BATTLE Michel
Poterie de la Montagne Noire, Route de
Saint-Ferreol, 31250 Revel
BEAUGRAND Philippe
'Le chat vert', 55, rue Basse, 59000 Lille
(20) 51 56 72
BERGER Alfred
5, rue de l'Observatoire,
67000 Strasbourg
(88) 61, 87. 52
Magasin Art-Al, Place des Tanneurs
BERSOUX Claude et Jean
97, rue Benoîte-Vincente, 62400 Bethune
(21) 25 28 88
BEREAU Christine
46, cours de la Republique et 5, rue
Camille-Dignac, 33470 Gujan-Mestras
BERTREMIEUX Sylviane
13, rue Beaumont, 59300 Valenciennes
BONNASSIES Paul
Rue des Potiers, 31220 Martres-Tolosane
(61) 90 81 49
BOUCRAUT Marie-Madeleine
16, passage d'Enfer, 75014 Paris
653 50 44
BRISY Jean
Hôtel de la Monnaie, 61, rue de la
Monnaie, 59000 Lille
(20) 51 85 19
BUCHHOLTZ Jacques
'Le Chartrou', 82110 Lauzerte
(63) 04 66 82
CASTILLON Patrick
264, bd de la Plage, 33120 Arcachon
CAUDRON Henri
15, place de la Vacquerie, 62000 Arras
(20) 21 14 23
'LES CERAMIQUES' (L. Y. Bonnet)
3, rue des Savonniers, 83400 Hyeres
(94) 65 40 10
CHAMPY Claude et Catherine
18, rue François-Coppée, 78370 Plaisir
639 10 44
CHATONEY Jean
Lou Darboun, 13960 Sausset-les-Pins
(42) 45 11 61
CHAUDET Josiane et SEYVE Yvonne

4, rue Gabriel-Rougier,
69370 Saint-Didier-du-Mont-d'Or
COLLET-FENETRIER
Rue Guy-Allard, 3850 Voiron
CORVAISIER Yaninka
3, rue Louis-Massotte, 78530 Buc
956 36 90
COVILLE J.
Impasse des Roses, 06410 Biot
DANIKOWSKI Boleslaw et Isabelle
Rue du Maeréchal-Lercler,
59310 Aix-les-Orchies
(20) 71 81 02
DELARUE
Route de Longfosse, 62240 Desvres
(21) 32 32 69
DELMOTTE Michel
9, rue des Dentelles, 67000 Strasbourg
(88) 32 57 44
DELOBAUX Jean
89, rue Saint-André, 59000 Lille
DERUELLE Véronique
31, rue Royale, 59000 Lille
(20) 93 91 50
DESCAMPS Didier
40, rue Etienne-Dolet,
59184 Sainghin-en-Weppes
(20) 58 57 80
FOURMANOIR Annie
37, bd Saint-Jacques, 75014 Paris
581 28 67
FRANCK France
47, rue Bonaparte, 75006 Paris
FROGER Jacky
'La Casette', Corps d'Uriage,
38410 Saint-Martin-d'Uriage
(76) 95 75 39
GONIN Florence
'Las Pastorale', Rue Claude-Monet,
78380 Bourgival
969 01 32
GOSSELINK Françoise et Willem
Côtes de Fumel, 82150 Valeilles
GRANET Alain
Montée Sainte-Anne, 06220 Vallauris
GUTMAN André
Sainte-Paule, 69620 Le Bois-d'Oingt
HIRLET Micehl et Andrée (by appt)
32, rue Claude-Terrasse, 75016 Paris
525 40 33
JAMMES Pierre
Zone artisanale, 12800 Nancelles
JUNG Dany
19, rue du Général-Leclerc,
67550 Vendenheim
(88) 69 51 64
KOSTANDA A.
42, av. G.-Clemenceau, 06220 Vallauris
LANDEPADAN et DIGNAT
31220 Martres-Tolosane
(61) 90 81 76

LECERF Jean
Argelies, 12150 Severac-le-Château
LEMPEREUR-LAUTE
Rue du Gal-Leclerc, 59216 Sars-Poteries
(20) 61 61 82.
LENTIER Roland
Route de Dimont, 59216 Sars-Poteries
(20) 61 63 49
L'HUILLIER Henriette
'Pepsy-Gres', 'La Vigue', 82150 Valeilles
(63) 04 48 98
De LOSOWITCH Patrick
12220 Montbazens
MARAIS Jean
'Le Caquelou', Rue des Fournas,
06220 Vallauris
(93) 63 85 74
MARTIN Geneviève
41, Grand-Rue, 78240 Chambourcy
965 28 41
MASSIP Michel
19, clos Maison-Blanche, Coignieres,
78310 Maurepas
050 31 58
MONTREAU Benoit et LOHOFF Elke
Arué, 40120 Roquefort
NEY Patrice
3, rue Anatole-France, 92370 Chaville
946 84 05.
NOEL Philippe
Rue de Strasbourg, 57155 Moyenvic
PALLOURE J.-J.
15, rue Edmond-Magnez,
78700 Conflans-Sainte-Honorine
972 40 12
PETIT Daniel
20, rue des Fusiliers-Marins,
67400 Eschau
(88) 64 14 45
PETTIT Olivier
Le Flayosquet, 83780 Flayosc
(94) 70 41 46
PICHON Odile et Loïc
43, rue Balard, 75015 Paris
578 90 90
PILLARD S.
Pérouges, 01800 Meximieux
(74) 61 01 27
PIRARD Vincent
16, rue du Fosse, 67620 Soufflenheim
(88) 36 57 62
PORTANIER Gilbert
Chemin des Potiers, 06220 Vallauris
POTERIE DES TROIS TERRES
(E. et C. Ploix)
A la sortie de l'agglomeration en
direction de Cogolin, 83360 Grimaud
(94) 43 21 62
RENAUDIN Kim
3, rue Gerard-de-Nerval,
38400 Saint-Martin-d'Heres

ROUART Philippe
97, avenue d'Italie, 75013 Paris
331 97 85
RUHLMANN Loys
39, rue des Potiers, 67660 Betschdorf
(88) 80 55 60
SARVER Daniel
20, rue Saint-Paul, 75004 Paris
274 52 07
STEFANOWSKI Didier
39, rue de la Republique,
12200 Villefranche-de-Rouergue
THIAM Claire et Michel
62, rue du Château-des-Princes, 54840
Gondreville
(83) 43 61 78
VAN LITH J.-P.
44 bis, rue Saint-Sébastien, 06410 Biot
(93) 65 13 47
VEREECKE Marcel
R.N. 344, 59120 Wallon-Cappell
(20) 41 71 34
VIANSON-PONTE Mme.
Château de Goussaincourt, 55140
Vaucouleurs
(29) 89 44 42
VOLLET Robert
Marchastel, 15400 Riom-es-Montagnes

## TEXTILES

L'ART DU CANEVAS (C. de
Lassagne)
22, quai Tilsitt, 69002 Lyon
(78) 37 20 33
L'ATELIER (Mme Dobrasz)
31, av. de la Forêt-Noire,
67000 Strasbourg
(88) 61 67 27
L'ATELIER DES BUCLOS
28, chemin de Chaumetière, 38240
Meylan
(76) 90 49 41
BELLEMIN Jacotte
5, rue Maret, 69540 Irigny (15 km au
sud de Lyon)
(78) 81 55 94
BERLIET André
59, montée de la Grande-Côte, (Atelier
49/51), 69001 Lyon
BIENFAIT Chantal
13, rue Jouvenet, 75016 Paris
525 83 55
BINAEPFEL Monique
Scharrachbergheim, 67310 Wasselonne
(88) 50 35 28
BLANC Françoise
'Le Poisson Soluble', 13, rue Raoul-
Blanchard, 38000 Grenoble

BONNEL Odette
32, place de l'Archevêche, 13100 Aix-en-
Provence, Sur rendez-vous
BRELET Catherine et Jean-Pierre
Câstel Jeanne-d'Arc, 83770 Seillans
(94) 76 05 26
BRUN Nicole
Quisqueya, Serre de Cazaux,
31800 Saint-Gaudens
(61) 89 21 90.
CHADEFAUX Dominique
Saint-Cirgues-de-Jordanne, 15590
Lascelle-Mandailles
CHARLIER Roger
11, av. Gambetta, 06600 Antibes
(93) 34 10 79
CHOQUET Jacqueline
10, rue de Beuvery, 78100 St-Germain-
en-Laye, 963 07 72.
COLSON Anne-Marie et Michel
Marciliargue, Chauffour-sur-Vell,
19500 Meyssac
DARTOIS Daniel
23, rue Tourat, 33000 Bordeaux
(56) 52 28 26
DAVID Jean-Claude
'Atelier de la Marmotte', 38960 Saint-
Etienne-du-Crossey, 'Filoselle et
Pétinoche', 13, place des Tilleuls (near
rue Bayard)
38000 Grenoble
DELORD Sylvie
1 bis, rue de Bondy,
19100 Brive-la-Gaillard
(55) 23 53 28
DORNSTETTER
4, rue de Shirmeck, 67570 Rothau
(88) 97 10 49
EL ATI Maricette
4, rue des Pucelles, 67000 Strasbourg
(88) 35 04 20
GALLISSAIRES Monique
25, avenue M.-Picon, 33550 Langoiran
GANDER Tisserand
3, rue Engel, 67600 Muttersholtz.
GELLENS Michel
'La Jars', Quaix-en-Chartreuse, 38000
Grenoble
GREMAUD Yvonne
'Atelier la Bura', 33, rue Berthe,
75018 Paris
252 17 59.
HUBERT Francine
4, rue des Etats, 54000 Nancy
41, rue du Four, 54840 Gondreville
(83) 43 62 40
HUSTER Annette
8, rue des Violettes, 78750 Mareil-Marly
958 27 31

LAGARDE Martine et Georges
40, Galerie de l'Arlequin, Apt. 1601,
38100 Grenoble
(76) 09 68 85
LANDON Bernadette
51, avenue de Paris, 78000 Versailles
951 77 05
LE MANACH Georges
'Manufacture des trous tours', 31, rue du
4-Septembre, 75002 Paris
073 64 67
LEPRETRE Carlos
46, rue Alexandre-Adam,
62200 Boulogne-sur-Mer
(21) 31 35 94
de LESDAIN Françoise
7, square d'Arcole, 78150 Le Chesnay
954 20 76
LIEBARD Marianne
22, clos Baron, 78112 Fourqueux
973 24 87
LLORY Annick
5, rue Saint-Pol-Roux,
78000 Guyancourt
LOGAN Liliane
Grand-rue et route de la Madeleine,
06490 Tourette-sur-Loup
(93) 59 36 14
LOPEZ DEL RIO Anne-Marie
11, rue Principale, Kaltenhouse,
67240 Bischwiller
MAGNIER Dany
'La Boulangerie', Rue Déodat-de-
Séverac, 31540 St-Félix-de-Lauragais
(61) 83 01 60
MAHU Danièle et Marcel
"La Jarrige", 19250 Meymac
(55) 72 41 20
MARTINOT Roger
5, rue Sellénick, 67000 Strasbourg
MEMHELD Dominique
1, rue Sainte-Odile, 67500 Haguenau
(88) 93 09 21
MICHAUD Jean-Claude
Les Mayons, 83340 Le Luc
MUNIER Jacqueline
114, rue Léonard-Bourcier, 54000 Nancy
(83) 96 14 00
NICAISE Josy
66, rue Esquermoise, 59000 Lille
(20) 31 81 06–31 42 04
NOTTER Jacky et Pierre
1, place de la Baleine, 69005 Lyon
(78) 37 72 76
PEREL Elyane
31, rue des Ursulines,
78100 St-Germain-en-Laye
963 01 93

PERRIN Yves
7, allée du Champ-d'Aisile,
Ste-Foy-les-Lyon
Atelier: 5, rue Longue, 69001 Lyon.
PINET Christiane
La Couertoirade, 12230 La Cavalerie
PROUVE Simone et SCHLOSSER
André
13, rue Titon, 75011 Paris
371 44 71
1, rue du Pont-Louis-Philippe,
75004 Paris
272 84 87
RIMBAULT-SAERENS
Place de l'Eglise, 83510 Lorgues
(94) 68 51 35
REBE
23, rue Danielle-Casanova, 75001 Paris
261 77 28
RENAU Nicole
La Margotton, Quartier Valcros,
13320 Bouc-Bel-Air
(91) 22 08 71
Sur rendez-vous.
RIOUX MARECHAL Elisabeth
'Le Colombier', Rue Gibier, Le
Mourillon, 83100 Toulon
RIPOCHE Marie-Paule
14, rue Pasteur, 62000 Arras
(21) 23 14 62
RISCH Paul
9, rue des Dentelles, 67000 Strasbourg
SABINE
L'Atelier du Tisserand, 81170 Cordes.
SANSONNET Odette
40, avenue Simon-Bolivar, 75019 Paris
205 85 76
SERRE Jacotte
8, rue du Puits-de-la-Grue,
95540 Méry-sur-Oise
036 43 95
SIDONIE
'Atelier Paris-Provence', 19, rue
Frédérick-Sauton, 75005 Paris
325 77 10
SULPICE Coryse
27, rue des Bigaudes,
78750 Mareil-Marly
958 06 48
LES TAPIS ET TISSUS DE
COGOLIN
Bd Louis-Blanc, 83310 Cogolin
(94) 43 40 45
Sur rendez-vous
TISSAGE PATRICIA
'La Moineaudière', La Rippe, Gleizé,
69400 Villefranche
(74) 68 31 02 ou 65 38 15
VALLAURI Pierre
Quartier des Baumouilles, 13710 Fuveau
(42) 58 71 81

# Index